NORTH DAKOTA

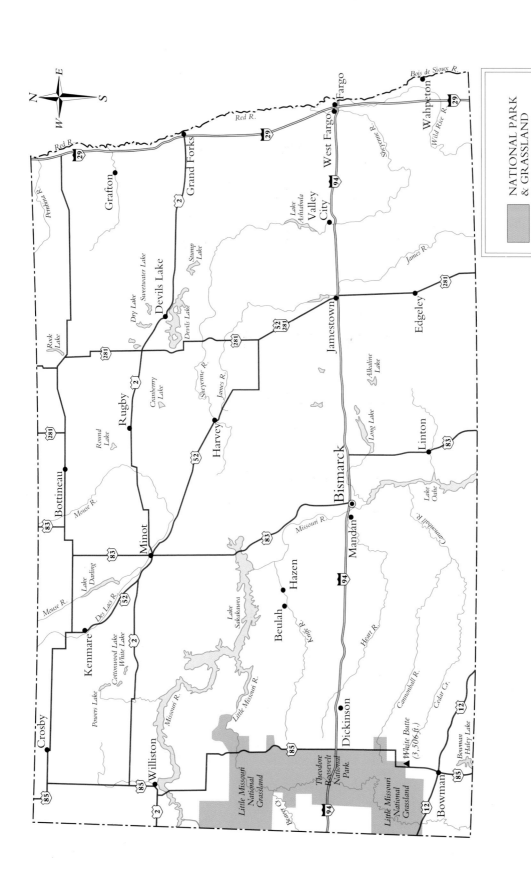

NORTH DAKOTA BY ROAD

NATIONAL PARK & GRASSLAND

MILES

0 10 20 30 40 50 60 70

CELEBRATE THE STATES
NORTH DAKOTA

Melissa McDaniel

BENCHMARK BOOKS

MARSHALL CAVENDISH
NEW YORK

For Jerry

Benchmark Books
Marshall Cavendish Corporation
99 White Plains Road
Tarrytown, New York 10591-9001

Copyright © 2001 by Marshall Cavendish Corporation

Library of Congress Cataloging-in-Publication Data
McDaniel, Melissa.
North Dakota / by Melissa McDaniel.
p. cm. – (Celebrate the States)
Includes bibliographical references and index.
ISBN 0-7614-1314-6
1. North Dakota—Juvenile literature. [1. North Dakota.]
I. Title. II. Series.
F636.3 .M38 2001   978.4—dc21   2001025964

Maps and graphics supplied by Oxford Cartographers, Oxford, England

Photo research by Ellen Barrett Dudley and Matthew J. Dudley

Cover photo: Corbis/Layne Kennedy

The photographs in this book are used by permission and through the courtesy of: *Corbis*: David Muench, 6-7,
107; Kevin Fleming, 10, 66-67, 123; Layne Kennedy, 13, 73, 96-97, 106; Annie Griffiths-Belt, 14,16, 19, 24,
25, 48, 53, 54, 57, 60, 61, 64, 70, 82-83; Tom Bean, 17; Steve Kaufman, 20, 114-115; Corbis, 36, 47;
Bettmann, 56, 94, 126, 127 (lower), 131; Lois Ellen Frank, 59; Richard Hamilton Smith, 69, 102; Richard A.
Cook, 77;   Roger Ressmeyer, 85; Underwood & Underwood, 90; Reuters New Media Inc., 92; Joe McDonald,
117 (right); George Lepp, 120 (right); Jeff Vanuga, 120 (left); AFP, 127 (top); Richard Schulman, 130; Hulton-
Deutch Collection, 132 (top); Andrew Cooper/Corbis Outline, 132 (lower); Phil Schermeister, back cover.
*North Dakota Tourism Department:*Dawn Charging, 22, 62, 72, 78, 104, 111; Clayton Wolt, 76, 125; Dan
Koeck, 99; Pat Hertz, 108; Bruce Wendt, 134. *Joslyn Art Museum, Omaha/ Enron Art Foundation:* 26-27.
National Museum of American Art, Washington DC/ Art Resource NY: 29. *State Historical Society of North Dakota:*
32, 34, 35, 38, 42, 44-45, 88. *Don Gienger,* 75. *Marc Norberg,* 86. *Photo Researchers Inc.:* Steinhart Aquarium,
117 (left). *Archive Photos:* 129.

Printed in Italy

1   3   5   6   4   2

CONTENTS

NORTH DAKOTA IS . . .

North Dakota is flat . . .

"The North Dakota prairie, when you see it for the first time, looks flatter and emptier than any landscape you have seen before. My mother used to say it was as if God had leveled it out with a rolling pin." —writer Richard Critchfield

. . . and it is empty . . .

"No matter which way you looked, you couldn't see a tree."
—Margaret Barthelemy, whose family moved to Mott in 1919

. . . except for the wheat.

"All you would need to paint [the] landscape would be gold for wheat and blue for sky." —writer Ian Frazier

North Dakota is a bit of a mystery to the rest of the nation . . .

"When I go back to New York, people say, 'North Dakota? Does that exist? You're from a state that doesn't exist.'"
—a motel owner who moved from New York City to Grand Forks

. . . and even to some North Dakotans.

"In the geography [book], among the pictures of Chicago's sky-line, Florida's palms, and the redwoods of California, there was one small snapshot of North Dakota. It showed a waving wheatfield. I could see *that* simply by turning my head to the sixth-grade window. Was that all there was, all we had? . . . Very early I acquired a sense of having no identity in the world, of inhabiting, by some cruel mistake, an outland, a lost and forgotten place upon the far horizon of my country." —journalist Eric Sevareid

But for those willing to stick it out, it's a great place to live . . .

"There's no crime. No violence. Saturday night in a bar—people spittin' on the floor—that's the only violence."
—Manard Meschke, longtime resident of Bowman

. . . and a great place to return to.

"I hadn't seen the stars for three or four years, my son couldn't play outside without always being supervised and then one time back in North Dakota I looked outside my window and there were some little guys, probably five or six years old, riding by with their bikes with fishing poles attached. That kind of decided it for me. So I moved back."
—lawyer Sarah Vogel, who returned to her home state after living in New York City

North Dakota is a land of flat farms and frigid winters, but it is many other things as well. North Dakota is brown buttes and green river valleys and wild, rugged badlands. It is pleasant towns, empty highways, and small but energetic cities. Most of all, it is friendly people. Come meet North Dakota.

1 QUIET BEAUTY

Journalist Eric Sevareid, a native of Velva, North Dakota, once called his home state "a large rectangular blank spot in the nation's mind." Indeed, most people know nothing about North Dakota's terrain except maybe that it's flat. But even that is only partly true.

THE EAST

The Red River valley, along North Dakota's eastern border with Minnesota, pretty much defines the word *flat*. Perfectly straight roads stretch to the horizon with no hills or bumps to hide them. Big white clouds float like cotton candy through the huge expanse of sky. The Red River valley has some of the best farmland in the world. During the summer it is a checkerboard of corn, wheat, sunflowers, and other crops. This fertile region is North Dakota's most densely populated area and includes two of the state's largest cities, Fargo and Grand Forks.

Heading west from the Red River, it isn't long before the perfect flatness disappears. In the north, you run into the Pembina and Turtle Mountains. Farther south, low hills appear. This area is sometimes called the prairie pothole region, because between these hills are thousands upon thousands of circular lakes and ponds that look like big potholes. Some of these lakes exist year-round, while others appear in the spring when the snow melts and then dry up by

North Dakota's prairie potholes provide birds with plenty of food and nesting spots.

the end of the summer. But small or large, they are all important, because these are where many ducks, geese, cranes, pelicans, and other birds breed. Thanks to these potholes, and the prairie grasses near them, more waterfowl are born in North Dakota than in any other state except Alaska.

THE WEST

Continuing west, you eventually come upon the wide, muddy expanse of the Missouri River. The Missouri starts in Montana and cuts across western North Dakota before turning south. After first seeing the Missouri River coursing between the towns of Bismarck and Mandan, novelist John Steinbeck wrote, "Here is where the map should fold. Here is the boundary between east and west. On the Bismarck side it is eastern landscape, eastern grass, with the look and the smell of eastern America. Across the Missouri on the Mandan side, it is pure west, with brown grass and water

More white pelicans nest at Chase Lake National Wildlife Refuge near Medina than anywhere else in North America.

LAND AND WATER

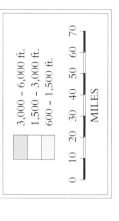

3,000 – 6,000 ft.
1,500 – 3,000 ft.
600 – 1,500 ft.

MILES

0 10 20 30 40 50 60 70

Crosby
Williston
Kenmare
Bottineau
Minot
Rugby
Grafton
Grand Forks
Devils Lake
Harvey
Valley City
Fargo
Wahpeton
Jamestown
Edgeley
Linton
Bismarck
Mandan
Hazen
Beulah
Dickinson
Bowman

White Butte
(3,506 ft.)

Red R.
Pembina R.
Red R.
Rock Lake
Mouse R.
Round Lake
Sweetwater Lake
Dry Lake
Devils Lake
Stump Lake
Cranberry Lake
Sheyenne R.
James R.
Lake Ashtabula
Sheyenne R.
Wild Rice R.
Bois de Sioux R.
James R.
Alkaline Lake
Long Lake
Lake Oahe
Cannonball R.
Rock
Missouri R.
Heart R.
Knife R.
Lake Sakakawea
Little Missouri R.
Missouri R.
Powers Lake
Cottonwood Lake
White Lake
Lake Darling
Des Lacs R.
Mouse R.
Cannonball R.
Cedar Cr.
Bowman Haley Lake
Beaver Cr.

"If you like empty space, North Dakota has real advantages," says writer Richard Critchfield.

scorings and small outcrops. The two sides of the river might as well be a thousand miles apart."

As you head into western North Dakota, the world grows browner. Crops give way to cows grazing on short, tough grass. Big brown bales of hay are everywhere. Buttes—steep isolated outcrops of land—dot the surrounding plain.

By the time you reach the badlands, in the southwestern corner of the state, you've entered another world. In this ruggedly beautiful region, wind and water have eroded the soft earth, leaving strange spires and domes. Water has etched sharp ravines into many of the formations. Trying to make his way through the badlands in 1864, General Alfred Sully called them "hell with the fires burned out."

In some places, the badlands do actually burn. Veins of a type of coal called lignite snake through the region. When lightning strikes the lignite, it sometimes catches fire. Lignite can burn for years and

President Theodore Roosevelt, who lived in North Dakota's badlands in the 1880s, once wrote "In much of the Bad Lands the buttes are so steep and broken that it needs genuine mountaineering skill to get through them."

years. The result is a red stripe called scoria. Other minerals have left stripes of gold, blue, silver, and brown in the earth. Theodore Roosevelt lived in the badlands before he became president. He once wrote that parts of it were "so fantastically broken in form and so bizarre in color as to seem hardly properly to belong to this earth."

WILD AND TAME

You won't see many trees in North Dakota. "If I see three trees in a row I get claustrophobic," jokes one North Dakotan. Before white settlers arrived, most of the state was empty prairie covered with wild grasses. In the west, the grasses were short, but in eastern North Dakota grasses could grow higher than a person's head. This sometimes proved deadly to the state's pioneers. Rachel Calouf, who moved to North Dakota from Russia in 1894, recalls getting lost in the grass: "There were no landmarks or lights. To lose your way on the prairie was like being lost at sea." Today, most of these majestic grasses have been plowed under, replaced by crops.

Less than 1 percent of North Dakota is forest, the smallest amount of any state. What forest the state does have is mostly found in the Turtle Mountains and Pembina Gorge, in the northeast. These woods of oak, aspen, and ash make pleasant homes for deer, beavers, cottontail rabbits, and even moose. Stands of cottonwood, willow, and elm thrive along riverbanks elsewhere in the state.

Although the badlands look harsh and barren, they are actually home to a wide variety of life. Hardy plants such as juniper trees and

Deer thrive throughout North Dakota.

prickly pear cactus cling to some slopes. Wood's rose, bluebells, and leopard lily bring color to the land in the spring. Prairie dogs pop out of holes in their "towns" between the jagged buttes, while deer and elk wander through the ravines. Porcupines, golden eagles, burrowing owls, horned toads, even buffalo—you'll find all sorts of creatures in the badlands.

Perch, catfish, carp, bass, walleye, and other fish fill North Dakota's lakes and rivers. One fish that hasn't fared so well is the pallid sturgeon. These fish, which have been around since the days of the dinosaurs, can live for sixty years and grow up to six feet long. They used to prowl the bottom of the Missouri River, hunting prey

Prairie dogs are a popular sight in the badlands.

in its rippling, turbulent water. But in the twentieth century, dams were built to control the Missouri's wild flow. Near Riverdale, North Dakota, massive Garrison Dam holds back the river's waters, forming Lake Sakakawea, the largest manmade lake entirely in one state. The dams on the Missouri prevent flooding, but they have been disastrous for the pallids. The shallow areas that young pallid sturgeon prefer have disappeared, and the river's water is so calm and clear that the pallids are robbed of their best hunting conditions. Today, only about 250 pallid sturgeon remain in the upper Missouri River. For the fish to survive there, some of their natural habitat will have to be restored. But this would mean letting the river's water level vary.

Many wild creatures that once lived in North Dakota—otters, grizzly bears, wolverines—have disappeared from the state as humans have tamed the land and water. Will the pallid sturgeon suffer the same fate? Only time will tell.

WILD WEATHER

Most people know that North Dakota is brutally cold in the winter. But what outsiders may not realize is that it is also scorchingly hot in the summer. And the wind, oh the wind. It blows so hard and steady that you have to shout to hear yourself think. Eric Sevareid once said it was "a trial of the human spirit just to live there, and a triumph of faith and fortitude for those who stayed on through the terrible blasting of the summer winds, the merciless suns, through the frozen darkness of winter."

Summers in North Dakota are generally clear and pleasant. But in the heart of the summer, temperatures frequently soar into the nineties. And with few trees to offer shade, the heat can be unbearable. One Oregonian recalled his first visit to North Dakota—"It was a hundred degrees and there were locusts everywhere"—and vowed never to return.

For an agricultural state, North Dakota is quite dry, averaging only seventeen inches of precipitation a year, and just thirteen inches in the west. The state's farmers get by because most of the rain comes

SLOW-MOTION FLOOD

Devils Lake is the largest natural lake in North Dakota, and it is getting bigger. Since 1993, it has risen twenty-five feet, tripling in size. In what amounts to a slow-motion flood, it has swallowed up houses and fields one at a time.

The lake has no natural outlet. So during times of heavy rain and snowfall, the water just keeps rising. This happened for much of the 1990s. About the only people happy about it are fishermen, who have never had it so good.

The federal and state governments have responded by elevating roads so they're above the water level and by moving people who live in harm's way. But North Dakotans are clamoring for a more permanent solution. They want canals built to drain the lake water into the Sheyenne River. From there it would flow into the Red River, which continues north into the Canadian province of Manitoba.

People have long dammed or diverted waters for their own use. Many people now believe this is unwise, because there are always unintended results. Manitobans worry that the striped bass or other creatures from Devils Lake, once released into the river, might devastate species in Canada. They also worry because Devils Lake has an unusually high salt content. This salty water might harm Canada's freshwater ecosystems.

Will solving one problem just create another? Larry Milian of the Manitoba Wildlife Federation believes so. "Mother Nature always has the last call," he says.

during late spring and summer, just when the crops need it. Much of it comes in crashing thunderstorms, when buckets of water pour down upon the earth.

North Dakota sees plenty of other extreme weather. Hailstorms crack windows and pound crops down to nothing. Droughts are a constant threat, as are floods. And tornadoes sometimes rip through the state, wreaking havoc.

When the wind kicks up, as it often does, North Dakota's weather can be even worse. The western Dakotas are the windiest part of the United States. With few trees or hills to block its way, the wind picks up speed as it rushes across the plains. It also picks up dust, snow, and anything else in its path, stinging the eyes, weathering the skin, and turning snowstorms into howling blizzards. "The wind in North Dakota is an almost living presence," wrote Robert P. Wilkins and Wynona Huchette Wilkins in their history of the state. "At the height of a prairie gale, it can blow a straw through a two-inch plank, propel snow through the tightest seam at window or door, and send dust through any man-made barrier."

Despite all this wild weather, it is the cold that North Dakota is famous for, and with good reason. North Dakota is one of the coldest states in the nation. In some places the temperature doesn't rise above freezing for months at a time, and temperatures below zero degrees Fahrenheit are common. "In cold like this," says novelist Larry Woiwode, "you don't breathe through your mouth or your lungs feel scorched."

Some North Dakotans lament their state's reputation as a frozen wasteland. "It seems to me unfortunate that we got the 'North' end of a very cold name," said Episcopal bishop Cameron Mann, who was trying to lure priests to the state in the early twentieth century. "I find that with each letter of the word 'North' a separate shiver seems to run along the spines of my hearers. They have visions of polar bears and icebergs."

In fact, people who live in North Dakota do get used to the cold. After a long cold spell, when the temperature creeps just a few degrees above zero, they act as if it's spring and take off their hats and gloves. Ultimately, enduring the cold becomes a point of pride for North Dakotans. They have a joke there: Forty below—keeps out the riff-raff.

North Dakotans get used to visitors asking, "Is it always this windy?"

"I pictured Siberia—a frozen wasteland with tons of snow," said a Tennessee
man on hearing that the air force was sending him to North Dakota.

2 YESTERDAY AND TODAY

Junction of the Yellowstone and the Missouri, *by Karl Bodmer*

Thousands of years ago, North Dakota looked very different from the way it looks today. Much of the land was covered with lush forest. Among the trees lived giant bison and huge beasts called mammoths and mastodons that were similar to today's elephants.

EARLY NORTH DAKOTANS

The first people arrived in North Dakota about 12,000 years go. These wandering people, called Paleo-Indians, survived by hunting the giant creatures that roamed the land. Eventually, the climate became drier. The forest turned to grassland and the large animals died off. As their main source of food disappeared, the people moved on.

In the centuries that followed, other people crisscrossed the region, gathering plants and hunting smaller bison and other animals that lived on the plains. These wandering hunters left behind spearpoints, tools, and other artifacts that have helped scientists better understand their cultures.

It wasn't until a thousand years ago that the tribes that live in North Dakota today first appeared in there. The first group to arrive was the Mandans. They established villages along the Missouri River, as did the Arikaras and Hidatsas. These groups adapted very well to life on the northern plains. For shelter, they built large,

The Mandan Indians lived in round earth lodges. Painting by George Catlin.

dome-shaped wooden frames and covered them with dirt to make earth lodges. In the rich land along the rivers, they planted fields of sunflowers, corn, squash, and beans. And in the vast grasslands, they hunted buffalo. They grew accustomed to the cold. Explorer

William Clark wrote that on a frigid January night they met Indians who had slept on the ground wearing only light clothes covered by a buffalo robe. They did not even light a fire to keep themselves warm.

The Ojibwa and the Sioux also moved into North Dakota. The Ojibwa settled in what is now North Dakota's northeastern corner, while the Sioux scattered across the plains. Both groups relied on the buffalo for their survival. The great beasts provided them with almost everything they needed. They used the meat for food, the skins for clothing and shelter, the bones for tools. And with 60 million buffalo spread out across the country, it seemed there would always be enough.

EXPLORERS AND TRADERS

By the time the Sioux had taken over the plains, the British and the French had established colonies in eastern North America. It was only a matter of time before they would want to see more of the continent. The first European known to have entered what is now North Dakota was a French Canadian named Pierre Gaultier de Varennes, Sieur de La Vérendrye. In 1738, he made it all the way to a Mandan village near present-day Bismarck before turning around and heading home.

Although a few other white men ventured south from Canada during the eighteenth century, none would have the impact of the first Americans to explore the region. In 1803, France sold the United States the Louisiana Purchase, a vast swath of land west of the Mississippi River. North Dakota was part of the bargain. In May

CURIOUS COYOTE: A SIOUX STORY

Here is one of the many Native American tales in which Coyote finds trouble.

One day Coyote was walking along when he met Rabbit, who was carrying a pouch on his back. "What have you got in that pouch?" Coyote asked.

"Nothing you would want," said Rabbit.

"Oh, you must have tobacco in that pouch," Coyote guessed. "I sure would like a smoke. Why don't you give me some."

Rabbit didn't answer.

"Oh, come on. Don't be so stingy," said Coyote.

Rabbit said nothing and kept on walking.

"Hey, Mr. Long-ears," Coyote shouted, "let me see what's in the pouch."

"It's nothing you would want," Rabbit said quietly.

"So let me see that nothing."

"No," said Rabbit. "You'd be mad at me."

Coyote couldn't stand it. His curiosity was killing him. Furious, he grabbed the pouch off Rabbit's back and opened it. The pouch was full of fleas, more than it was possible to count. As the mass of fleas settled on Coyote, he tore off across the field, scratching himself and howling.

"I told you so," Rabbit shouted after him.

Ever since then, every night you'll hear coyotes howl. They howl because the fleas are still biting them and they itch like mad.

The first Europeans to enter North Dakota were fur trappers and traders.

1804, Meriwether Lewis and William Clark left St. Louis, Missouri, to explore the Louisiana Purchase. Their mission was to find a route to the Pacific Ocean and learn all they could about the plants, animals, and Indians along the way.

Lewis and Clark's party spent months slowly making their way up the Missouri River. By the time they reached North Dakota it was autumn, and they began looking for a place to spend the winter. On October 23, they met the Mandans. "They are the most friendly, well disposed Indians inhabiting the Missouri. They are brave, humane and hospitable," Clark wrote. The explorers built a fort near the Mandan and Hidatsa villages north of present-day Washburn.

During that long, cold winter at Fort Mandan they met Sacagawea, a young Shoshone woman. She, her husband, and their infant son traveled with Lewis and Clark on the rest of their voyage to the Pacific. During the trip, Sacagawea proved very useful to the explorers, helping them pass safely through Shoshone territory, saving important papers that fell overboard, and showing them which plants were safe to eat.

Lewis and Clark passed through North Dakota again in 1806 as they went back east to tell the world of the vast and bountiful lands out west.

In the years between La Vérendrye's and Lewis and Clark's journeys, fur traders made their way into North Dakota from Canada. They traded knives, guns, blankets, sugar, coffee, alcohol, and other goods to the Indians in exchange for beaver and buffalo pelts. They built trading posts all along the Red and Missouri Rivers.

One of the first was constructed near present-day Pembina in northeastern North Dakota. In 1812, a group of farmers moved south from Canada and settled nearby. They built crude log cabins and turned Pembina into North Dakota's first permanent European settlement. They toughed it out for a few years, but most eventually returned to Canada. Those who remained were known

Fort Union, on the western edge of what is now North Dakota, was the busiest trading post on the Great Plains. Between six and eight hundred buffalo were killed every year to feed the people who worked there.

as métis—the families of French-Canadian fur traders who had married Ojibwa and Cree Indian women.

BROKEN PROMISES

For several decades, North Dakota remained primarily the home of Native Americans. But over time, contact with white Americans increased until it changed their world forever.

Some of the early traders and explorers exposed the Indians to

THE MÉTIS

With one foot in European culture and the other in Native American culture, the métis borrowed from both traditions to forge their own unique way of life.

The métis spoke a combination of French and Indian languages and wore a combination of French and Indian dress. The men wore blue cloaks with leather leggings, moccasins, and sashes around their waists. They often decorated their clothing with feathers, beads, and gold braids.

The métis economy was based on the buffalo hunt and the fur trade. Twice a year all the métis in North Dakota, Minnesota, and Canada gathered for a huge buffalo hunt in which they killed tens of thousands of animals. They were, explorer Joseph Nicollet wrote in 1839, "the best hunters, the most expert horsemen, and the bravest warriors of the prairies."

diseases they had never encountered before. In 1837, smallpox spread quickly through Indian villages. By the time the outbreak was over, only about 150 Mandans and 500 Hidatsas remained.

Later in the century, whites began slaughtering buffalo to make way for railroads and settlers. Railroads sent special trains filled with professional hunters out onto the plains. Shooting at the shaggy beasts from the windows of the train, one man could kill hundreds a day, leaving the bodies to rot on the plains. By 1889, only 541 buffalo remained in the entire country. Without the buffalo, the Indians could not sustain their traditional way of life.

The railroads hired professional hunters to slaughter buffalo.

The U.S. government had made treaties promising the Indians that certain areas would remain Indian territory—that whites would not settle there. But as more people pushed out onto the prairies, the treaties were broken. By 1882, North Dakota's Indians had been forced onto four reservations, where they eked out an existence and tried to keep their cultures alive.

SETTLING THE PRAIRIE

Meriwether Lewis had called northern Dakota "one of the fairest portions of the globe" and described it as "fertile, well-watered, and intersected by such a number of navigable streams." But many others who ventured out from the East Coast were not impressed. Nothing but desert, they said, not suitable for settlement or farming.

In 1861, the U.S. Congress created Dakota Territory, which included present-day North and South Dakota, as well as parts of Montana and Wyoming. Two years later, the Homestead Act went into effect. This law offered 160 acres of free land to anyone who lived on their claim for five years. But northern Dakota was considered so unappealing that even this generous offer failed to lure many people. By 1870, only twenty-eight settlers had filed homestead claims there.

It was the railroad that ultimately opened up North Dakota. In 1872, the Northern Pacific Railroad began laying track across northern Dakota. At last there would be an easy way to move people and goods across the vast prairie.

Railroad officials were among the first to take advantage of this.

To encourage the Northern Pacific Railroad to build across the plains, the U.S. government gave the company huge swaths of land around the tracks. The Northern Pacific ended up owning one-quarter of North Dakota.

George W. Cass and Benjamin Cheney of the Northern Pacific established a huge wheat farm in the Red River valley. They hoped it would be so successful that it would draw other people to the area. Sure enough, they were soon swimming in profits. Before long, other corporations and wealthy families also set up massive farms, some so large the rows of wheat stretched for six miles. These spreads earned so much money that they became known as bonanza farms. Meanwhile, on the other side of what would become North Dakota, cattle ranching was taking off.

Still, the vast majority of northern Dakota remained unsettled. To lure settlers, the government and the railroads advertised all over the eastern United States and western Europe. They stressed the cheap land, while failing to mention the harsh weather. They also wildly exaggerated the land's fertility. "Scratch the soil and the finest crops spring up. Thrust a shrub in the earth and it bears fruit," wrote one North Dakota official.

In much of Europe, land was scarce and poverty persistent. The offer sounded too good to pass up. Immigrants began pouring in from Norway, Germany, Russia, Sweden, and many other places. The Great Dakota Boom was on.

Although the government gave the pioneers land, that didn't mean life was easy. The first problem was building a house. The Homestead Act required that the settlers build at least a twelve-by-fourteen-foot claim shack in order to get title to the land. But when you're living on an empty prairie with no tree in sight, how do you build a house? Many people looked to the land beneath their feet. They cut blocks of earth, or sod, from the ground and stacked them up to make a simple dwelling. These sod houses stayed cool in the

DAKOTA LAND

North Dakota's early settlers found a rich but difficult land. It took all their strength to make a go of it. But they didn't lose their sense of humor, as this parody of the old hymn "Beulah Land" shows.

Music: "Beulah Land"

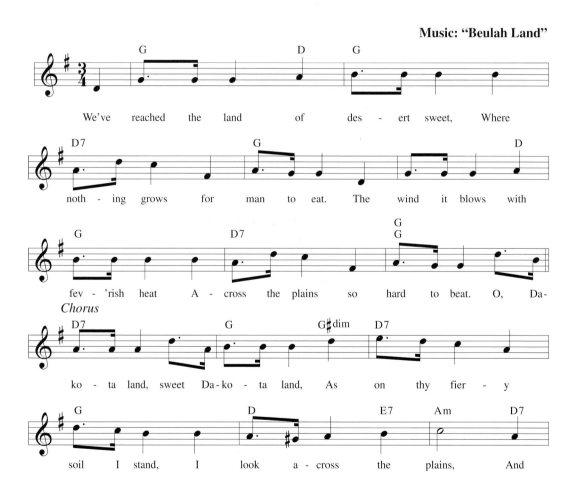

We've reached the land of des - ert sweet, Where
noth - ing grows for man to eat. The wind it blows with
fev - 'rish heat A - cross the plains so hard to beat. O, Da-

Chorus

ko - ta land, sweet Da - ko - ta land, As on thy fier - y
soil I stand, I look a - cross the plains, And

won - der why it nev - er rains, Till Ga - briel blows his

trum - pet sound, And says the rain's just gone a - round.

We've reached the land of hills and stones.
Where all is strewn with buffalo bones.
O, buffalo bones, bleached buffalo bones,
I seem to hear your sighs and moans. *Chorus*

We have no wheat, we have no oats,
We have no corn to feeds our shoats.
Our chickens are so very poor,
They beg for crumbs outside the door. *Chorus*

Our horses are the bronco race,
Starvation stares them in the face.
We do not live, we only stay,
We are too poor to get away. *Chorus*

Homesteading was a lonely life. Quilting parties gave pioneer women welcome company.

summer and warm in the winter and could withstand the vicious prairie wind.

Building a claim shack was just the beginning of the home-steaders' trials. Farming the land sometimes seemed impossible. Drought, hail, and prairie fires were constant threats. In some years swarms of grasshoppers appeared and ate all the crops in a single day. But for many people, isolation was the most unbearable part of homesteading, especially during the long, frigid winters. "My mother didn't see another woman between September and May," recalls one woman who grew up in Mott. For other people, the prairie itself was overwhelming. There was "too much of everything," said one homesteader. "Too much sky, too much horizon, and definitely too much virgin, bleak prairie land in all directions."

By the end of the century, railroad tracks crisscrossed the state, and towns sprouted along the rails. They were lively, bustling places, full of hope and promise. Newspapers, stores, banks, and churches lined the streets. One fellow reported that in Linton "the stores are open until midnight. . . . The hotel where there were several beds in each room [had] several people in each bed."

In 1870, just 2,405 white people lived in northern Dakota. By 1890, the year after North Dakota became a state, that number had jumped to 191,000. By 1910, it had ballooned to 577,000. More than 70 percent were immigrants or the children of immigrants, the highest percentage in the nation at that time.

THE NONPARTISAN LEAGUE

Many people who flooded into North Dakota eventually had their dreams dashed. The bonanza farmers went broke when wheat prices plummeted in 1890. Ranchers soon discovered that the badlands weren't the ideal place to graze cattle. If the cows didn't die of thirst during the scorching summers, they might freeze to death during the frigid winters. And less than half of the homesteaders managed to stick it out the required five years.

Those who stayed continued to face hardships. Railroads, grain companies, and banks took big bites out of farmers' profits, sometimes leaving them deep in debt. The frustrated farmers finally united in 1915, when Arthur C. Townley founded the Nonpartisan League (NPL). The NPL called for state-owned banks to provide farmers with low-interest loans and state-owned flour mills that would charge lower fees. Within a year 40,000 farmers had joined the NPL.

Nonpartisan League candidates soon won almost all state offices. Many of their reforms were passed, such as spending more money on rural schools and giving farmers tax breaks. The state also founded the Bank of North Dakota and the North Dakota Mill and

Elevator, which still operate today. Over time, the NPL's influence waned. It eventually merged with the Democratic Party.

DROUGHT AND DESPERATION

Although the NPL did what it could to help farmers, there was little it could do in the 1920s, when North Dakota's economy went into a tailspin. The price of wheat plunged, farmers went broke, banks failed, and people lost their savings. By 1929, the Great Depression plagued the entire country.

The Great Depression hit North Dakota hard. Between 1932 and 1937, the state's income per person was just 47 percent of the national average.

To make matters worse, throughout the early 1930s a devastating drought gripped the center of the nation. Year after year, the sun beat down. Eventually the land became so dry that much of it just blew away. Huge clouds of dust swept across the plains, burying fences and piling up against the sides of buildings. One North Dakotan recalled, "The dust got so bad you'd have to put lamps on to see inside the house. It got that bad."

The worst year for North Dakotans was 1936, the hottest and driest year on record. No wheat at all was harvested in most North Dakota counties that year. By the decade's end, a third of North Dakota farmers had lost their land. Thinking nothing remained for them there, tens of thousands of people left the state in the 1930s.

Most people who stayed needed help from the government to survive. The government sponsored construction projects to put people back to work. Although it was a hard time for everybody, the state ended up with highways, bridges, and buildings that would serve its citizens for decades.

UPS AND DOWNS

The drought had ended by the time the United States entered World War II in 1941. North Dakota farmers bounced back with record wheat harvests to supply the armed forces with food.

But the rebound wouldn't last for long. Wheat prices dropped again by the decade's end. And as machinery performed more and more farm tasks, fewer workers were needed. So even more people left the land. Some began a new life in North Dakota's cities. Many others gave up on North Dakota entirely.

When North Dakota's new capitol was built in the 1930s, it dominated the landscape.

During the last half-century, North Dakota continued to have ups and downs. Wheat prices rose and fell. Blizzards, drought, and floods took their toll. And people continued to leave the countryside. Some found jobs when oil was discovered in the western part of the state in 1951. But they soon discovered that oil was no more reliable a source of income than wheat. As North Dakota heads into the twenty-first century, it continues to struggle with how to broaden its economy. Only then will people be able to stay and work in the state they love.

3 WORKING TOGETHER

The capitol in Bismarck

In 1936, a South Dakotan wrote, "North Dakota has taken up and enthusiastically endorsed more crackpot political schemes than any other two states." Today, politics in North Dakota is much calmer, as people in Bismarck, the state capital, go about their business of providing the state's citizens with good schools and safe streets.

INSIDE GOVERNMENT

North Dakota is still governed by its original constitution of 1889. Like the U.S. government, the state government is divided into three branches—executive, legislative, and judicial.

Executive. The executive branch makes sure that North Dakota's laws are enforced. The head of the executive branch is the governor, who serves a four-year term. He or she appoints important officials and submits a budget to the state legislature. The governor also signs bills passed by the legislature to make them law or vetoes bills to reject them.

The other executive branch officials are the lieutenant governor, attorney general, secretary of state, treasurer, auditor, superintendent of public instruction, and the commissioners of agriculture, insurance, and taxation.

Legislative. The North Dakota legislature is made up of a forty-nine-member senate and a ninety-eight-member house of

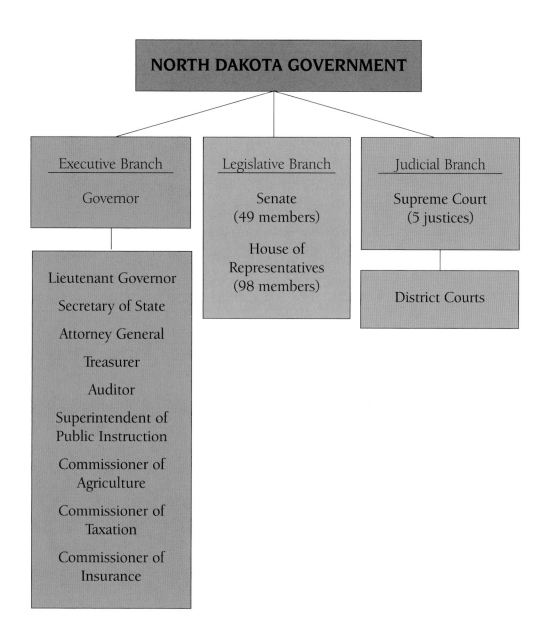

NORTH DAKOTA GOVERNMENT

Executive Branch

Governor

Lieutenant Governor

Secretary of State

Attorney General

Treasurer

Auditor

Superintendent of
Public Instruction

Commissioner of
Agriculture

Commissioner of
Taxation

Commissioner of
Insurance

Legislative Branch

Senate
(49 members)

House of
Representatives
(98 members)

Judicial Branch

Supreme Court
(5 justices)

District Courts

representatives. Senators and representatives are both elected to four-year terms. Legislators propose new laws and make changes to old ones. Once a proposed law, called a bill, is passed in both the house and the senate, it is sent to the governor for approval. But even if the governor vetoes a bill, it can still become law if two-thirds of the members of each house vote to approve it again.

Judicial. Most trials in North Dakota are held in district courts. The people of North Dakota elect forty-two district court judges to six-year terms. If someone thinks an error was made in a trial, he or she can ask the state supreme court to review the case. The North Dakota Supreme Court consists of five justices elected to ten-year terms. Besides handling appeals from district courts, the supreme court also rules on whether laws violate the state constitution.

EDUCATION

One word that has been buzzing around Bismarck lately is *education*. North Dakotans are proud of their school system and with good reason. Test scores are high, and they have the lowest drop out rate in the country. But there are also problems. North Dakota has the second-lowest teacher salaries in the nation. Wages are so low that many teachers are lured away to other parts of the country, and some schools have had trouble filling positions. In 2000, John Hoeven successfully ran for governor by promising to improve teacher pay. The following year a law was passed giving all teachers in the state an extra three thousand dollars a year.

A more complex problem is school consolidation. Back when North Dakota was mostly rural, each little town had a thriving school. But as families left the countryside, the number of kids in these schools dwindled until the schools could hardly keep their doors open.

The state government has long encouraged small schools to

North Dakotans are struggling to find ways to keep good teachers in the state.

merge. State officials argue that it wastes money to keep schools open that serve only a handful of students, since it requires many more teachers and administrators to run several small schools than one large one. They also claim that tiny schools don't offer children the same educational opportunities as larger schools, such as advanced science equipment and special art classes.

But people in North Dakota's smallest communities point out that in small schools, children get more attention. The grade school in Robinson has three teachers for just twelve students. "We have what rich people pay for," says Gene Hetletved, the Robinson school board president. And many parents don't like the idea of sending their children on hour-long bus rides to schools in distant towns, especially during the icy winter. Plus, in many small towns, schools are much more than a place to educate children. They often function as community centers, where meetings and social events take place. "The school *is* the town," says Heidi Schatz, one of two seniors in the last graduating class in Butte.

It is not unusual for some rural schools in North Dakota to have only two graduates in a year.

The North Dakota legislature passed a law offering money to school districts that merge. When this didn't work, it passed a law that allows school construction only in districts where the number of students is steady or rising. So far, nothing the state has done has made much difference. Although officials in Bismarck believe that school consolidation is best for everyone, it is going to be a long, slow process. Most small North Dakota towns are determined to hold on to their schools as long as possible.

MAKING A LIVING

Although only about 8 percent of North Dakotans work on farms these days, agriculture is still the heart of North Dakota's economy. Wheat was the first crop to take hold in North Dakota, and it remains the most important. North Dakota produces more wheat

GROSS STATE PRODUCT: $17.9 BILLION

(2000 estimated)

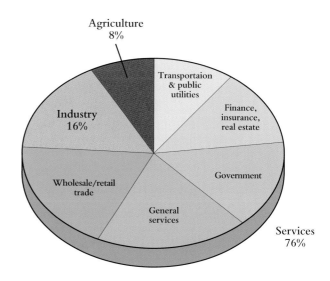

Agriculture
8%

Transportaion
& public
utilities

Finance,
insurance,
real estate

Industry
16%

Government

Wholesale/retail
trade

General
services

Services
76%

North Dakota farmers produce enough wheat each year to make 114 billion sandwiches.

than any other state. But unlike a century ago, today North Dakota farmers also raise many other crops. North Dakota leads the nation in growing barley, sunflower seeds, and flax. Sugar beets and potatoes flourish in the fertile Red River valley. Farther west where it is drier, farmers produce oats and hay.

Much of this hay is used to feed cattle, which graze on North Dakota's western plains. Nearly a million calves are born in North Dakota each year. The state's ranchers also raise hogs, sheep, and turkeys. Some even keep bees—North Dakota ranks among the nation's top honey producers.

Farming is in the blood of many North Dakotans. They grew up on the land, and they can't imagine a better life. "I like to be out here in the peace and quiet," says one farmer from Portland. "You're your own boss."

But farming is a hard business. North Dakota farmers struggle to hold on, but prices fall, droughts and floods destroy crops, and each

Cattle are the most important livestock in North Dakota.

EARNING A LIVING

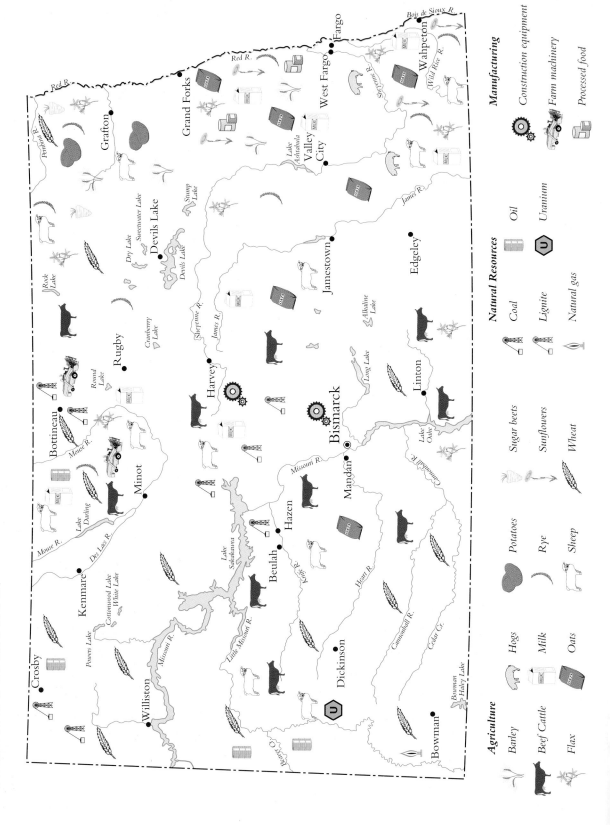

Manufacturing

- ⚙ Construction equipment
- 🚜 Farm machinery
- 📦 Processed food

Natural Resources

- ⛏ Coal
- ⛏ Lignite
- Ⓤ Uranium
- 🛢 Oil
- 🔥 Natural gas

Agriculture

- 🌾 Barley
- 🐄 Beef Cattle
- 🌾 Flax
- 🐷 Hogs
- 🥛 Milk
- 🌾 Oats
- 🥔 Potatoes
- 🌾 Rye
- 🐑 Sheep
- 🥬 Sugar beets
- 🌻 Sunflowers
- 🌾 Wheat

RECIPE: DAKOTA FLAPJACKS

Many North Dakotans like a hearty breakfast. Practically all the ingredients for these filling flapjacks are produced in North Dakota. Have an adult help you with this recipe.

1 cup whole wheat flour
¾ cup white flour
⅓ cup cornmeal
¼ cup rolled oats
2 tbsp. sugar
2 tsp. baking powder
1 tsp. salt
½ tsp. baking soda
1¼ cup milk
4 tbsp. melted butter
¼ cup honey
3 eggs

Mix the dry ingredients in one bowl and the wet ingredients in another. Pour the wet ingredients over the dry ingredients and mix them together. Place a skillet or griddle on the stovetop over medium heat and grease it lightly with oil or butter. Pour ¼ cup of the batter for each flapjack, leaving 4 or 5 inches between each so they have room to spread. Cook until bubbles appear on the top of each flapjack and then flip them. Cook a bit more until the bottom is just brown. Then take your flapjacks off the griddle, top them off with North Dakota honey, and dig in.

In 1933, North Dakota was home to 86,000 farms. Today there are just 30,000.

year they owe more money. Every year more people give up, abandoning their dreams that one day their children will take over the farm. And as more and more farmers leave, the small-town grocery stores and hardware stores and cafes and tractor dealerships that serve them also close up shop. "We don't have anything now," says Marabeth Hunter of the little town of Mountain. "Just the one

North Dakota leads the nation in the production of honey.

Each summer, North Dakota shows off its farming talent at the North Dakota State Fair in Minot. Farmers enter their cows, pigs, sheep, and even stalks of wheat to see who has raised the most perfect specimen. Everything from cakes to quilts to tractors is on display. Exhibits with unusual farm animals such as ostriches are particularly appealing. "Mama, this little one—he was eating my pants," says an excited boy at a pygmy goat stall. "But it's okay, 'cause he's got real tiny teeth." If admiring animals isn't your thing, try the monster truck derby or the cooking demonstrations, the carnival rides or the camel rides. Music, rodeos, clowns—the list goes on and on. Which is to say, every one of the quarter million people who attend the fair each year find something to entertain them.

bar, the cafe that's open half days, the old folks home and the church. I wish we had stores here, at least one. You have to run sixteen miles to get milk." And so the stream of people to the cities continues.

In the cities, job prospects are brighter. Manufacturing is now as important to North Dakota's economy as agriculture. Food processing tops the list of the state's many industries. It makes sense. All those agricultural products grown in North Dakota need to be turned into food products. Wheat becomes pasta, seeds are pressed into cooking oil. The Aviko company turns potatoes into 240 million pounds of french fries every year and sells them to restaurants like Wendy's. North Dakota also manufactures a lot of farm machinery. But not everything made in North Dakota is related to agriculture. Construction equipment and airplane parts are made in the state, as are computer disks and software.

Although oil isn't the booming industry that it once was in western North Dakota, some oil wells in western North Dakota are still pumping. Coal, clay, sand and gravel, and salt are also coaxed from the ground in North Dakota.

But most people in North Dakota, like most people in the rest of the country, work in service industries. This means that rather than growing or building something, people perform a service. Many North Dakotans work in schools, banks, stores, hospitals, and military bases.

The biggest problem with many jobs in North Dakota is that they don't pay much. Many service jobs pay only six or seven dollars an hour, not enough to pay the bills. "My husband is a rancher. My son is a plumber and he works with my husband," says a motel

The area around Williston, North Dakota, enjoyed an oil boom in the 1970s. Some of these rigs are still pumping.

clerk in Stanley. "You have to have two jobs to make it." North Dakota is tied with Montana in having the highest percentage of workers who have more than one job.

North Dakota's low wages have an upside, however. Companies

have found that they can get well-educated, spirited workers in North Dakota at much lower wages than they pay in big cities. Using computers, telephones, and the Internet, North Dakotans can answer customers' questions or book plane reservations or keep files up-to-date for companies that are based half a continent away.

One of the first people to take advantage of this was Hal Rosenbluth, who runs a large travel company in Pennsylvania. In 1988, he set up a small office in a closed tractor store in Linton. He soon found that North Dakota's former farmers and store clerks were far more reliable and efficient than his employees in the East. Today, Rosenbluth International employs more than a thousand North Dakotans, who are happy to have secure jobs with benefits.

Rosenbluth is certain that with their people skills and modern technology, North Dakotans can attract more and more of this kind of business. "You need to blend high tech and high touch," he tells them. "Go out in the world and strut your stuff."

4 PRAIRIE PEOPLE

In 1910, Theodore Roosevelt told a crowd in Fargo, "If it had not been for what I learned during those years that I spent here in North Dakota, I would never have been president of the United States." Over the years, many people have found that it takes resilience and resourcefulness to make it in North Dakota, but that the effort is worth it.

GOOD NEIGHBORS

North Dakotans prize their quality of life. People are friendly and helpful. Walk into any store and you'll get a big smile and a "how ya doin'?" Rusty Findley, an air force colonel based in Grand Forks, finds this friendly attitude refreshing. "The people in the local community have good values, and they're down to earth," he says. "Most go out of their way to help families ease their stay up here." Anyone who has ever found themselves stuck by the side of the road with a flat tire can attest to North Dakotans' helpfulness. "Most places I've been stationed," says another air force officer, "people will whiz past you at seventy miles an hour and beep their horn to boot." But in North Dakota, someone will always stop and help.

North Dakota has one of the lowest crime rates in the country, so people feel safe. "Last night, eleven o'clock, I went out for a walk for an hour all around," says a Grand Forks woman, who moved to

North Dakotans pride themselves on being good neighbors. One man says, "If you're a farmer and you break your leg today at work, you're going to have ten neighbors coming in to [harvest your fields], free of charge."

the state from New York City. "No problem." This sense of security is what draws many people to the state. "It's better for kids," says the same woman. "It's peaceful here. You don't lock the house. You don't lock the car." In fact, during the winter, when it's hard to get cars started, many people leave their car running with the keys in the ignition while they go shopping or have dinner. They never worry about whether their car will still be there when they come back. One fellow recalls leaving his cell phone in a restaurant. Three hours later, when he realized he had forgotten it, he rushed back. It was there on the table, exactly where he had left it. "People here are good, honest folk," he said.

SMALL TOWNS AND CITIES

Some think the people of North Dakota are honest and friendly because its cities and towns are small, so everybody knows everybody else. "If you go and you're a rat, everybody in town knows you're a rat; they treat you like a rat," says a man from Prairie.

But North Dakota isn't for everyone. "Too hot, too buggy, too boring," says a Bismarck woman one August. Even Fargo, the largest

Many North Dakotans who leave the countryside end up in Fargo.

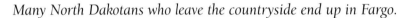

POPULATION GROWTH: 1880–2000

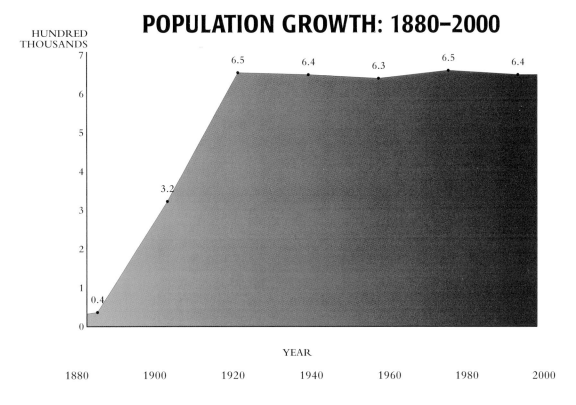

HUNDRED THOUSANDS

7

6

5

4

3

2

1

0

6.5   6.4   6.3   6.5   6.4

3.2

0.4

YEAR

1880   1900   1920   1940   1960   1980   2000

city in North Dakota, has only 90,000 people. It just doesn't have the same variety—of foods, of stores, of art, of people—that a big city has. And small towns provide even fewer options. "Walhalla doesn't have anything to offer young people," says one woman of her town in the state's northeastern corner. "It's got none of the glitz and glamour." She says kids growing up can't wait to head off to Minneapolis, Minnesota, the nearest big city.

But for people who love clean air and no traffic, who like both to have a little elbow room and to know their neighbors, small-town North Dakota is the place to be. "This place is big enough

A beautiful day on Lake Sakakawea

for me," says Orella Sylling of tiny Hamberg. "I could never live in a bigger town."

OUTDOOR FUN

With all its wide-open spaces, North Dakota offers plenty of outdoor activities. Fishing is one of the most popular. On weekends,

Lake Sakakawea is filled with boaters dangling lines. The Red River is one of the country's best catfish spots. Devils Lake is another fishing hot spot. No matter what part of North Dakota they live in, people can always find some peaceful stretch of water where they can wait for a bite. "It's cleansing, almost spiritual for me," says one avid fisherman. "If I'm having a bad day, I come down to the river and clear my head."

Other people prefer hiking or horseback riding through the

Horseback riding is a thrill in North Dakota's wide-open spaces.

prairies and badlands. Mountain bikers were thrilled when a 120-mile trail that runs down along creek bottoms and up over buttes and even through cow pastures opened in the badlands in 1998. "One fella on a tractor waved us down," Dale Heglund, one of the first bikers to use the trail, said happily. "He had never seen a mountain bike before and wanted to see what kind of guys ride those things!"

When winter descends, many people settle down in their living room with a good book. But others refuse to come inside. Instead, they get out their snowmobiles or their skis. Some skiers head to cross-country trails, but in places like the Pembina Gorge, North Dakota has steep enough terrain to offer downhill skiing. Even anglers can stay active in the winter. During the darkest, coldest days, they drive out onto frozen lakes, cut a hole in the ice, drop a line through the hole, and wait for walleye or perch to bite. The state's biggest ice fishing gathering happens each January on Devils Lake, when 2,500 people head onto the ice at once to see who can catch the biggest fish.

OLD-TIMERS AND NEWCOMERS

Native Americans lived in North Dakota long before Europeans began settling there. Today, American Indians are the largest minority group in the state, making up 5 percent of the population. Each year, tribes across the state host powwows. These celebrations are filled with dancing, drumming, and food. They help keep traditions alive and give old friends a chance to catch up. The United Tribes International Powwow, held in Bismarck each September, is one of

READY, SET, MOW!

On a sunny Saturday in Mandan, North Dakota, the air crackles with excitement as hundreds of people look out across a dirt race track. When the announcer says, "On your mark, get set, get ready, mow!" a bunch of burly men run to their lawn mowers, hop on, and put the pedal to the metal.

Lawn mower racing is probably the strangest sport ever to catch on in North Dakota. One reason for its popularity is that it's cheap. Unlike cars, old mowers can be had for a song, so everybody can live out their dream of being a race car driver. Richard Bohlman of Tioga uses a mower nearly thirty years old. "My uncle bought it for me when I was twelve to mow the grass on my grandfather's farm," he says. By the time the racers have fixed them up, the mowers can zip along at sixty miles an hour instead of the five they might do in the backyard.

Lawn mower racing isn't for the faint of heart. Plenty of people spin out or pop wheelies and tip over. The racers wear helmets for good reason.

What started out in the 1970s as a Fourth of July contest is on the road to becoming an organized sport. There are lawn mower racing circuits, and newspapers report on the action. One thing lawn mower racing doesn't have yet is prize money. Says Bruce Kaufman, the president of the United States Lawn Mower Racing Association, "We race for trophies, bragging rights, and glory."

Snowmobiling is just one way North Dakotans enjoy their long winters.

the nation's top powwows. Native Americans come from all over the country to dance together and display their artwork.

Today, the vast majority of North Dakotans were born in the United States, but not so long ago immigrants streamed into the state. In fact, at the dawn of the twentieth century, North Dakota was the most multicultural state in the nation, with the highest proportion of foreign-born residents of any state. The largest groups were Norwegians, Germans, English, and Irish. But Greeks, Swedes, Armenians, Poles, Finns, Bulgarians, and others each established their own communities. Groups of Russian Jews settled on the prairie outside of Bismarck and Devils Lake. Lebanese Muslims built a mosque near Minot.

Dancing is at the heart of most powwows.

ETHNIC NORTH DAKOTA

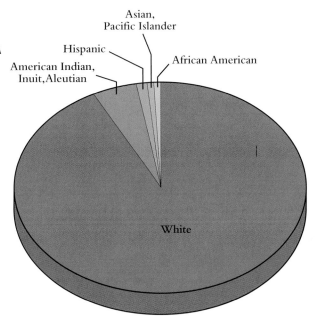

American Indian, Inuit, Aleutian

Hispanic

Asian, Pacific Islander

African American

White

Today, many North Dakota towns still bear signs of the groups that founded them. Walk around the cemetery in the town of Mountain and you'll see that many of the tombstones have Icelandic writing on them. Even today, Mountain, with a population of 120, is the largest Icelandic settlement outside of Iceland. Each year, many North Dakota towns hold celebrations to honor their heritage. At events such as Dickinson's Ukrainian Festival and New Leipzig's Oktoberfest, everyone in town gathers to enjoy traditional food, music, and dancing.

In recent years, North Dakota has seen an influx of people from

A young woman celebrates her family's heritage at the Ukrainian Festival in Dickinson.

NEARLY NORWAY

Did you ever want to taste that Scandinavian delicacy Arctic reindeer? Or how about lutefisk—codfish soaked in lye and then boiled? One place you can try these foods is at Norsk Hostfest, the nation's biggest Scandinavian festival, which is held in Minot each October.

Back in the late nineteenth and early twentieth centuries, immigrants from Scandinavian countries such as Norway and Sweden poured into North Dakota to start a new life. Today, some of their descendants believe that Norsk Hostfest is the best place to pay tribute to their roots. "It's as close as you can get to Norway without actually getting on a plane and flying," says one visitor.

Besides digging into the amazing array of food, the festival's 60,000 visitors spend a lot of time admiring traditional arts and crafts such as rosemaling, flowery decorations painted on wood. On one of the festival's five stages they might hear American country music legend Willie Nelson or Norway's leading male country singer Bjoro Haaland. Other musicians wander the crowd playing traditional instruments such as the five-foot-long Swedish horn called the lur.

"You have to remember where you came from, that's the beginning of all knowledge" says one fairgoer dressed like a Scandinavian warrior from centuries ago. "Hostfest reminds you."

beyond Europe. Some Mexicans who came to pick fruits and vegetables during the summer have made the state their permanent home. And people from China, the Philippines, Vietnam, India, and many other nations have made new lives for themselves in North Dakota.

Although immigrants to North Dakota once spread out across the prairie, today they are more likely to settle in the cities. Fargo, in particular, has welcomed a lot of newcomers. Many are refugees from troubled places around the world, such as Somalia, Bosnia, the Sudan, Zaire, Cambodia, Haiti, and Iraq. Today, Fargo schools welcome children who speak more than twenty different languages.

For people who have spent many desperate years in refugee camps, Fargo's quiet streets are a godsend. These immigrants appreciate the good schools, the low crime rate, and North Dakotans' generosity. And the people of Fargo have grown accustomed to their new neighbors. "We used to get a lot of looks," says Fowsia Adde, who wears the colorful scarves and dresses traditionally worn by Somali women. "Now, people are used to us." Although the newcomers like their new home, most are committed to keeping their own religions and customs in the predominantly Christian, white town. "We want to be American," says Dahir Sharif-Ahmed, another Somali. "But we also don't want to give up our own culture."

5 FAMOUS FOLK

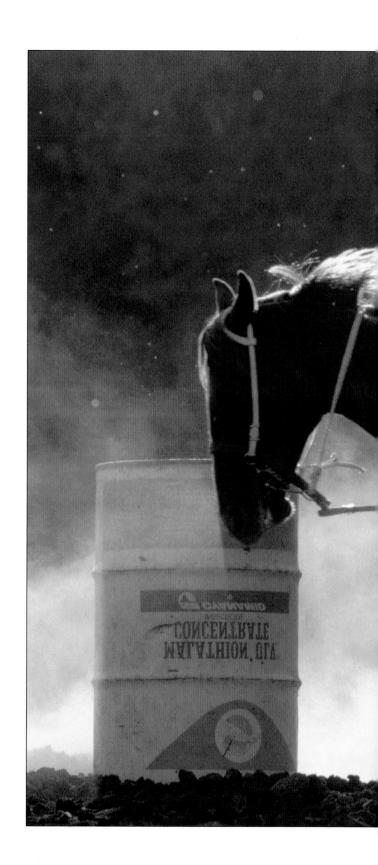

North Dakota has the fourth-lowest population of the fifty states. But out of the sparsely settled prairies have come some amazing people.

CAPTURING THE WEST

The all-time best-selling writer of westerns grew up on the North Dakota prairie. Louis L'Amour was born in Jamestown in 1908, the son of a farm-machinery salesman who was also Jamestown's chief of police. L'Amour read constantly as a child, and he couldn't wait to get out and see the world. He left home at fifteen and wandered the West. Over the next few years, he worked as a miner and a lumberjack, a circus hand and a hay baler. And through it all he listened, absorbing the stories and attitudes of the people he met. "Sitting around cow camps and in mining towns, I listened more than I talked," L'Amour recalled. "The men and women I met were survivors. Some survived by skill, some by chance."

When he started writing westerns in the 1950s, the people he had met found their way into his stories. L'Amour wrote romantic tales of resilient and upstanding young men who forge ahead and survive. In book after book—*Hondo*, *High Lonesome*, *Sackett*—they start out loners and turn into settlers. L'Amour had an abiding love for the brave people who settled the West, and for the land itself.

"The men who came West were . . . the pick of the country," Louis L'Amour once said. "I want to show where they came from, how the West influenced them and what they became."

He once wrote, "I have always wished I could have been the first man west, or one of the first to ride or walk in that country when only the Indians were there, to see it unblemished, unchanged, in all its original beauty. I came too late for that, so I wrote a story about a man who did."

By his death in 1988, L'Amour had written more than a hundred books. More than 200 million copies of his books have been sold, making him one of the most successful novelists of all time.

Novelist Louise Erdrich has a different perspective on the West.

Louise Erdrich comes from a family of storytellers. "People just sit and the stories start coming, one after another," she says. "You just sort of grab the tail end of the last person's story: It reminds you of something and you keep going on."

Erdrich is part Ojibwa. Both her parents worked at the school for Indians in the Red River valley town of Wahpeton, where she grew up. As a child, she often visited her mother's relatives on the

Turtle Mountain Reservation in the northern part of the state. She was particularly impressed by her grandfather, who was tribal chairman for many years.

Erdrich's first novel, *Love Medicine*, was published in 1984 to great acclaim. Like her later books, it is set in the stark North Dakota landscape. Many of Erdrich's characters share her mixed heritage. "This was part of my life—it wasn't something that I was making up," Erdrich once said. "I didn't choose the material; it chose me." Her characters move from the reservation to the city and back again, looking for love and a place in the world. Some never find either, but they endure. Out of their funny and tragic hard-luck stories comes a complex vision of modern Indian life.

OVER THE POLE

Back when airplanes were still a new invention, many people thought they would never be of much use. They were good for stunts and useful in wars, but few dreamed that planes would one day be used for everyday travel. In the 1920s, aviators set about proving just what airplanes could do. One such pioneer was Carl Ben Eielson, who gained fame for his Arctic adventures.

Eielson was born in Hatton, North Dakota, in 1897. Fascinated by planes from childhood, he got his first flying experience during World War I. After the war, Eielson returned home and started barnstorming—flying around the countryside, performing stunts and giving people rides.

A teaching job took Eielson to Alaska. He quickly realized that aviation could be particularly useful there because the region's vast frozen terrain made other forms of travel difficult. Soon he was delivering people, supplies, and mail to isolated communities. A trip that would have taken weeks by dogsled took just hours in Eielson's plane.

Eielson's skill at flying in the frozen north caught the attention of Australian explorer Hubert Wilkins, who wanted to explore the

Carl Ben Eielson was the first person to fly over both the North and the South Poles.

Arctic by air. Wilkins hired Eielson to fly him over the North Pole.

In 1926, they took off on their dangerous mission. A ferocious blizzard soon forced them to turn back, but Eielson had become the first person to fly out over the Arctic Ocean. They headed out again the following year, but this time engine trouble forced them down, making Eielson the first person ever to land a plane on floating ice. By the third emergency landing of the day the plane had run out of gas. Eielson and Wilkins had no choice but to make the return journey on foot. After twelve days and 125 miles, they finally reached a trading post. Their trek is considered one of the greatest feats of Arctic survival of all time.

Although Eielson lost a finger to frostbite during the harrowing experience, he didn't let that stop him. In 1928, the two set off again, and this time they made it over the Pole all the way to Norway. Awards and adulation rained down upon them. Later that same year, they made an expedition to Antarctica, at the other end of the world.

This was Eielson's last great adventure. In 1929, a ship got stuck in the ice along the coast of Siberia, across the Bering Strait from Alaska. Eielson and his mechanic took off in a raging blizzard to try to rescue the passengers. They never made it. The world had lost its best Arctic pilot. In recognition of Eielson's courage and achievement in bringing air travel to Alaska, both a mountain and an air force base there are named after him.

SINGING SOFTLY

At the height of her career, Peggy Lee practically whispered. Early on, the jazz and pop star had learned that the quieter she sang,

One critic said of Peggy Lee's cool, quiet voice, "Never has so much been delivered from so little."

the more people paid attention—and the more she was able to express.

Peggy Lee was born in Jamestown in 1920, where she grew up singing in church choirs. As soon as she graduated from high school, she headed for Hollywood to find fame and fortune.

Instead, she soon found herself working as a waitress, so she returned to North Dakota and began singing at a radio station in Fargo. Other gigs soon followed, and in 1941 she was discovered by Benny Goodman, the leader of the country's most popular swing band.

By then she had developed the soft, cool, almost purring style that would make her famous. For the next two decades Lee's sultry delivery of songs such as "Fever" made her one of the nation's most popular performers. Unlike many singers of the day, Lee wrote many of her biggest hits, including "Mañana" and "It's a Good Day." She even wrote some of the songs—and provided some of the voices—for the animated film *Lady and the Tramp*.

Lee continued to perform into the 1990s. "I've been easy on my voice. . . . That's why I'm still around," she said late in her career. "Besides, if you shout, you can't converse with your audience, and that's what I do best."

THE QUIET COACH

Most coaches in the National Basketball Association (NBA) stomp up and down the sidelines, yelling at the players. But not Phil Jackson. He sits there quietly, letting his players play. This relaxed style has made him one of the most successful coaches in the NBA.

Phil Jackson was born in Montana, the son of ministers. His family moved frequently during his childhood, until finally settling down in Williston, North Dakota. By high school, he was a basketball whiz, leading his team to the state championship. After playing college ball at the University of North Dakota, Jackson went

Phil Jackson is quiet but extremely competitive.

to New York to play for the Knicks for eleven years.

When his career as an athlete was winding down, Jackson began looking for coaching jobs. He had trouble finding them, however, perhaps because of his reputation. "Jackson was known as a flake," says sportswriter Sam Smith, "which is the general NBA definition of anyone who reads something other than the sports pages on the road. He read philosophy and religion."

After many years working as an assistant and coaching in a minor league, Jackson finally became the head coach of the Chicago Bulls in 1989. The Bulls were led by Michael Jordan, the best player in the game, but they relied on him too much. Jackson worked up a team strategy that got all the players involved. Once they were on the court, he let the players manage the details, rather than always calling plays as some coaches do. In his first year as head coach, the Bulls made it to the NBA semifinals. The next year they won the championship. They went on to win five more championships in the next seven years.

Jackson later became coach of the Los Angeles Lakers, who, like the Bulls, had superstars who had failed to gel as a team. "I'm no savior," Jackson said after he took the job. "They have to be the savior of themselves." Once again, Jackson proved himself a great leader and motivator, in his own low-key way. The team won the championship his first year there.

THE HOME RUN KING

Even though for thirty-seven years Roger Maris held baseball's record for the most home runs in a single season, he always had a hard time getting the respect he deserved. Some people resented him for surpassing the legendary Babe Ruth's record. Other people wished that his New York Yankee teammate Mickey Mantle—a more colorful, glamorous figure—had broken the record. But it was the quiet North Dakotan who ended up in the record books.

Roger Maris grew up in Fargo. He was an active child, always itching to get outside. He loved hockey and became a star football

"You know, '61 was an easy season," Roger Maris once recalled. "It was fun. It was exciting. How could it not be?"

player. He was offered a football scholarship to the University of Oklahoma, but when a Cleveland Indians scout spotted him, he jumped at the chance to play professional baseball instead.

By 1960, Maris was playing for the Yankees. He and Mantle were an incredible duo, leaving pitchers quaking in their shoes. That year Maris hit thirty-nine home runs to Mantle's forty, but it was Maris who took home the league's Most Valuable Player Award.

In 1961, Maris was hitting home runs at an even more blistering clip. As the summer wore on, he was on a pace to surpass Babe Ruth's record of sixty home runs in 1927. Every day the pressure mounted. Maris, an intensely private man, grew weary of the spotlight. "I'm sick of all this," he said as he inched ever nearer to the record. "I wish I were home with my wife and kids. I can't wait for this season to end." The press, who couldn't get enough of him the year before, turned on him, calling him a whiner. But Maris persevered. On the last day of the season he hit number sixty-one, a record that would stand until 1998, when Mark McGwire smashed seventy homers.

Roger Maris was probably the most famous person ever to come out of North Dakota. "I can't even tell you who might be in second place," says one Fargoan. "Roger's ours. Always was, always will be. Gives us a reason to stick out our chests and feel proud."

6 DISCOVER NORTH DAKOTA

Northo Dakota is not the first place most people think of when they are planning a vacation. In fact, it's the least visited of the fifty United States. But if you're willing to go off the beaten path and discover North Dakota for yourself, you'll find it is full of fascinating people and places.

THE RED RIVER VALLEY

Let's start our tour in the east, the most populated part of North Dakota. Although small by many states' standards, Fargo is North Dakota's biggest city. Among the highlights of its lively downtown is the Plains Art Museum, which is the largest fine arts museum between Minneapolis, Minnesota, and Seattle, Washington. Housed in a beautifully converted old warehouse, this airy museum specializes in Indian art and works by plains painters.

In the town of West Fargo is a different kind of museum, one dedicated to preserving North Dakota's past. Historic buildings from around the county have been moved to Bonanzaville U.S.A. There's a barber shop from Buffalo, a one-room schoolhouse from Mapleton Township, a lovely Lutheran church from Horace, and Fargo's first house. Built in 1869, the house has served over the years as a hotel and a jail. Bonanzaville also shows off hundred-year-old cars and horse-drawn farm equipment. The best time to

Visitors to Bonanzaville U.S.A. can get a taste of the nineteenth century.

visit is during Pioneer Days in August, when you can see fiddlers and candlemakers, weavers and threshers all in action.

Heading west puts you in the flat, checkerboard land of the Red River valley. Driving down its perfectly straight roads past tidy fields is strangely peaceful. Nothing seems to be moving but the cloud of dust thrown up by a pickup bouncing down a dirt road. The small towns you pass through are also unusually quiet. Oftentimes many of the stores are boarded up. All that remains open are a gas station, a couple of insurance offices, a cafe, and a grain elevator looming above it all.

TEN LARGEST CITIES

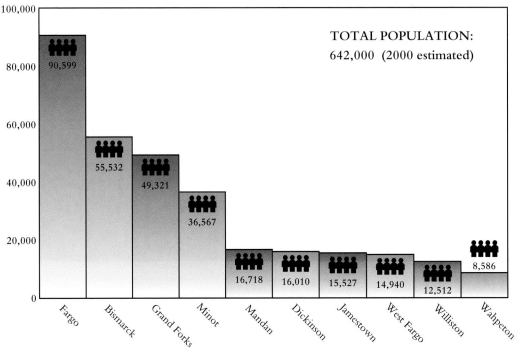

TOTAL POPULATION:
642,000 (2000 estimated)

POPULATION

Fargo	90,599
Bismarck	55,532
Grand Forks	49,321
Minot	36,567
Mandan	16,718
Dickinson	16,010
Jamestown	15,527
West Fargo	14,940
Williston	12,512
Wahpeton	8,586

One site worth visiting in this austere landscape is the KTHI television tower near Blanchard. At 2,063 feet, it's the tallest structure in North America. Gazing up at its swaying height is dizzying. You feel grateful for the huge cables stretching far out into the surrounding fields that keep it steady.

THE PRAIRIE POTHOLE REGION

If you keep going west you soon find yourself in the prairie pothole region. Water laps at both sides of the road and telephone poles

PLACES TO SEE

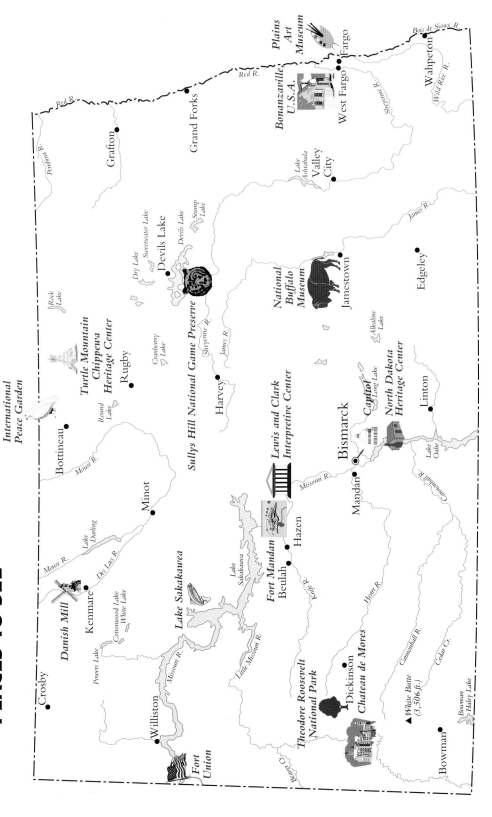

International
Peace Garden

Crosby

Danish Mill

Kenmare

Williston

Fort
Union

Lake Sakakawea

Theodore Roosevelt
National Park

Dickinson

Chateau de Mores

▲ White Butte
(3,506 ft.)

Bowman

Bottineau

Minot

Mouse R.

Mouse R.

Lake
Darling

Des Lac R.

Powers Lake

Cottonwood Lake
White Lake

Missouri R.

Little Missouri R.

Lake
Sakakawea

Knife R.

Beaver Cr.

Heart R.

Cannonball R.

Cedar Cr.

Bowman
Haley Lake

Rock
Lake

Round
Lake

Rugby

Turtle Mountain
Chippewa
Heritage Center

Dry Lake

Sweetwater Lake

Cranberry
Lake

Devils Lake

Sullys Hill National Game Preserve

Harvey

Sheyenne R.

James R.

Fort Mandan

Beulah

Hazen

Lewis and Clark
Interpretive Center

Missouri R.

Mandan

Bismarck

Capitol

North Dakota
Heritage Center

Lake
Oahe

Cannonball R.

Linton

Long Lake

Alkaline
Lake

Devils Lake

Stump
Lake

National
Buffalo
Museum

Jamestown

Edgeley

James R.

Pembina R.

Red R.

Grafton

Red R.

Grand Forks

Lake
Ashtabula

Valley
City

Sheyenne R.

Bonanzaville
U.S.A.

West Fargo

Plains
Art
Museum

Fargo

Bois de Sioux R.

Wahpeton

Wild Rice R.

stick up out of lakes that will be dry by summer's end. Birds are everywhere. Over every little hill is another lake with another row of baby ducks swimming behind their mother. The prairie pothole region is an area of subtle beauty and small triumphs: If you get on State Route 46, you can drive 110 miles without turning the steering wheel. It's the longest stretch of highway in the country without a single curve.

Most people who head to Jamestown have one thing on their

Writer Richard Critchfield grew up in North Dakota. "I often found it startling, going back in recent years," he says. "The fierceness of the light, the enormity of the blue prairie sky, the perfectly flat, unbroken plain visible between the houses and down every street."

minds: buffalo. Jamestown is the proud home of what it calls the world's largest buffalo, a forty-six-foot-long sculpture made of concrete and steel. Although it's impressive to be able to walk under a giant buffalo's nose, seeing the real thing is even better. You can do that at the National Buffalo Museum. The museum boasts a herd that includes a white buffalo named White Cloud. White buffalos are considered sacred by some Native Americans, a sign of peace and hope. After checking out the mighty creatures, you can go inside the museum to see artifacts such as buffalo robes and tools made from buffalo bone.

North Dakota is home to more wildlife refuges than any other state. One of the most accessible is Sullys Hill National Game Preserve, just south of Devils Lake, which has been set aside as a home for bison and elk. On a drive or hike through the refuge, you might spy these magnificent creatures, along with foxes, rabbits, minks, or eagles. In the winter, folks come to the refuge to take advantage of its cross-country ski trails, which lead skiers through the peaceful, pristine countryside.

Driving north, you might want to head off the main road to stand at the geographical center of North America. A stone monument marks the exact middle of the continent. After being in the center of things, get back on the highway and head for the beautiful International Peace Garden. The garden straddles the border between the United States and Canada, honoring the peace and friendship of the two countries. It is filled with brilliant flowers, including some that decorate an eighteen-foot-wide clock. The garden is an ideal place for hiking, biking, picnicking, and camping. It is also home to the International Music Camp, where young people from dozens of

countries hone their talents every summer. If you're lucky, you might catch one of their concerts.

Not far from the International Peace Garden is the Turtle Mountain Indian Reservation. In Belcourt, the reservation's main city, the Turtle Mountain Chippewa Heritage Center has displays about the history and culture of the Ojibwa people (who are also called Chippewa). Particularly interesting are the paintings and crafts that blend ancient traditions and modern styles.

LEWIS AND CLARK COUNTRY

On their voyage of discovery, Lewis and Clark traveled up the Missouri River, which winds through the heart of North Dakota. Traveling along that river today, you'll find many reminders of their journey. At the Lewis and Clark Interpretive Center in Washburn, exhibits cover everything from the clothes the travelers wore to the music they played. You can see a canoe like the ones they built to carry goods up the river or try on a buffalo-skin robe. Nearby is a reconstruction of Fort Mandan, where Lewis and Clark spent the first winter of their journey. Visitors can explore the simple log buildings that sheltered the explorers from the frigid cold.

The history at the Knife River Indian Villages National Historic Site goes back much farther. Scientists have found pieces of tools and

The International Peace Garden honors the friendship between the United States and Canada.

THE WORLD'S LARGEST . . .

Thousands of years ago, huge woolly mammoths and mastodons roamed the region that would become North Dakota. These animals have long since died out, but today other giant creatures loom over the landscape.

The world's largest Holstein cow—thirty-eight feet tall and made of steel and fiberglass—stands guard over New Salem. The world's largest sandhill crane towers over Steele. Then there's the twenty-foot-high gorilla in Harvey. And don't forget the forty-foot grasshopper, the twenty-six-foot-long walleye, or the gigantic turtle made from two thousand tires.

Sometimes it seems North Dakotans will do just about anything to make motorists pull off the state's long, lonely highways. "People drive up and they laugh and laugh at the bird," says Susie White, owner of a motel near the giant sandhill crane. "But they're stopping and that's what's important."

Many of North Dakota's incredible creatures weren't built to attract tourists. So the question is: Why?

Perhaps the long North Dakota winters have left some folks with a little too much time on their hands. A visitor to the world's largest buffalo in Jamestown has another idea: "Maybe they're compensating for a lack of mountains."

other artifacts there that are thousands of years old. The Hidatsas began building earth lodges on the site five hundred years before Lewis and Clark passed through. One of these lodges has been reconstructed. It's an impressive sight—fifty feet across and twenty feet high. The interior is warm and spacious, large enough to house a couple dozen people. Spread around the room are backrests, pottery,

Fort Mandan, where Lewis and Clark spent the first winter of their historic voyage, has been reconstructed.

A statue of Sacagawea, who met Lewis and Clark during their winter in North Dakota, graces the capitol grounds in Bismarck.

baskets, and other items that would have been in the lodge. Outside, in the quiet along the river, are indentations in the ground where hundreds of these lodges once stood, the most obvious sign of the proud people who once lived here.

Farther south is Bismarck, the state capital. Your first stop should be the capitol building itself. A nineteen-story tower, it is one of only four skyscraper capitols in the nation. It was built in the 1930s, after fire engulfed the state's more traditional first capitol. The pleasant capitol grounds contain a nature trail and statues that reflect North Dakota's history, including Sacagawea, a buffalo, a pioneer family, and a horse.

While visiting Bismarck, make sure you leave plenty of time for the North Dakota Heritage Center. This excellent museum covers the breadth of North Dakota history, from ancient animals to modern life. A magnificent collection of Indian clothing, pottery, and other artifacts is on display. Homesteaders' struggles are brought to life with exhibits that include everything from tools to toys. Letters written to the families they left behind capture the hope and desperation of pioneer life.

After all this history, it might be time to get outdoors and play a little. Luckily, Lake Sakakawea isn't far off. The lake is famed as a fishing spot, especially for catching walleye. But if you don't like to fish, you can go swimming, windsurfing, or sailing. Or you might want to just kick back, relax, and watch the light bounce off the ripples in the water. No matter what you do, you're bound to be refreshed after spending a day at the lake.

INTO THE WEST

Western North Dakota has a lot of long, lonely stretches of road. Hills rise up in strange shapes near rivers and then recede behind you. Rows of clouds line up in the big blue bowl of a sky.

There's not a lot to pull you off the highway in the northwestern part of the state. But one town that makes a pleasant rest stop is Kenmare, the perfect example of small-town North Dakota's quiet beauty. "My parents come here for their vacations," says one resident. "They say it's peaceful here and they can get away from the hustle and bustle of the city. And it's true! They go berry picking and ride their bikes and watch the birds." At the center of town is a pretty park with a windmill. The bright red Danish Mill was built by a Danish immigrant in 1902. For decades it was used to grind wheat into flour. Today, it is a good reminder of how recent North Dakota's pioneer past is.

In the early nineteenth century, trading posts were built all along the upper Missouri River. The most important was Fort Union, near where the Yellowstone River flows into the Missouri. A hundred people worked at the fort—cooks, cattlemen, traders, blacksmiths, hunters, and interpreters—and many others passed through. Indians, Russians, African Americans, Spaniards, Italians, and Frenchmen all mingled in the fort. "Until it was abandoned in 1867," says writer Ian Frazier. "Fort Union was like the Times Square of the plains."

Today, much of the fort has been reconstructed. You can tour the fancy Bourgeois House, where the superintendent of the fort lived, and the more modest Indian trade house where Native Americans brought pelts to trade for pans, knives, cloth, and other goods. The

Fort Union is dominated by the lavish Bourgeois House. Though it was at the far reaches of the frontier, people who ate dinner at the house were required to wear a jacket.

RIDE 'EM COWBOY

Ridin', ropin', brandin'. For anyone who has ever dreamed of being a cowboy, the Knife River Ranch is the place to go.

All across the West, dude ranches cater to city folks who want to saddle up horses under the big western sky. But Ron Wanner's ranch in the rugged hills of western North Dakota is one of the few places where visitors do real ranch work on a real working ranch.

Depending on what needs to be done, guests might help with a cattle drive, give animals shots, or even take a turn with the branding iron. "I didn't know you could hurt so much and be alive," remarked one guest with a smile after a long day of chores.

Of course visitors also have the chance to ride horses through the wide-open countryside, do a little fishing, and chow down at a steak fry. But it's the satisfaction of a job well done that makes them want to return.

"I'm almost 47 years old and this is something in my whole life I never thought I'd do," says one enthusiastic guest. "Ron gives everyone a job, and you feel like you're a real member of the team. By the end of the day, I felt like I'd been driving cows all my life."

walls of the trade shop are stocked with all the items that would have been available 150 years ago. Park rangers decked out in the clothes of the time are happy to tell visitors colorful stories about the fort and the fur trade. They may even offer you a hot drink that's been warming over the fire in the huge fireplace.

Many adventurers and travelers passed through Fort Union, including Karl Bodmer and George Catlin, both famous for their paintings of Native Americans and the West. The area around the

fort—the wide unruly Missouri and the peaceful empty plai
still looks remarkably like their paintings.

Southwestern North Dakota is home to the badlands, the most
spectacular part of the state. Before heading for the scenic vistas,
many people stop by the town of Medora to absorb some of its
Old West flavor. Medora was named for the wife of the Marquis de
Mores, a French nobleman who founded the town. He came to the
badlands in 1883 with the dream of making a killing in the cattle
industry. His scheme collapsed before it even got started, and
in 1886 he returned to France. He left behind a lavish house,
the Chateau de Mores. You can tour the house to learn all about the
man and his grand plans.

The heart of the badlands is Theodore Roosevelt National Park.
Roads lead visitors among the fantastic formations, past multicolored
domes and buttes and broken cliffs. But to really appreciate the
rugged land, you need to get out of the car. Even a short hike will
make apparent the incredible variety of plants that survive in the
harsh environment. And you never know when you might come over
a rise and see a deer or an elk or even one of the wild horses that
live in the park.

To experience the park at its best, spend the night there. As the
sun fades, the spires and domes become even more unearthly. In
the absolute darkness, the stars are amazingly bright. And there's
nothing quite like waking up in the morning to the twittering of
birds and peeking out of the tent to see buffalo chomping on grass
nearby. It's the perfect end to a trip through North Dakota.

Over: Wild horses roam some parts of Theodore Roosevelt National Park.

THE FLAG: *The North Dakota state flag was adopted in 1911. It shows a version of the coat of arms of the United States against a dark blue background.*

THE SEAL: *On the state seal, symbols of agriculture, including a plow and a blacksmith's anvil, surround a tree in an open field. An Indian on horseback hunting a buffalo represents North Dakota's Native American heritage. The seal was adopted in 1889.*

STATE SURVEY

Statehood: November 2, 1889

Origin of Name: North Dakota takes its name from the Sioux Indians, who are also known as the Lakota or Dakota, meaning "friend."

Nicknames: Flickertail State, Roughrider State, Peace Garden State

Capital: Bismarck

Motto: Liberty and Union Now and Forever, One and Inseparable

Bird: Western meadowlark

Fish: Northern pike

Flower: Wild prairie rose

Grass: Western wheatgrass

Western meadowlark

Northern pike

NORTH DAKOTA HYMN

Adopted as the official state song in 1947.

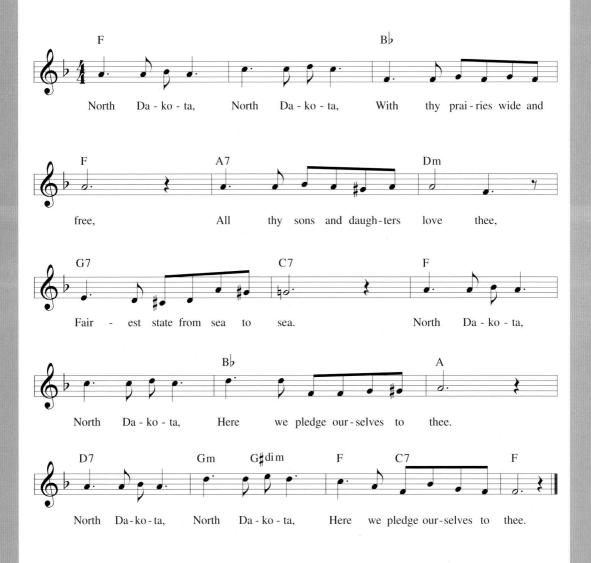

Tree: American elm

Fossil: Teredo petrified wood

Beverage: Milk

Dance: Square dance

GEOGRAPHY

Highest Point: 3,506 feet above sea level, at White Butte

Lowest Point: 750 feet above sea level, on the Red River

Area: 70,704 square miles

Greatest Distance, North to South: 212 miles

Greatest Distance, East to West: 360 miles

Bordering States: Montana to the west, South Dakota to the south, Minnesota to the east

Hottest Recorded Temperature: 121°F at Steele on July 6, 1936

Coldest Recorded Temperature: –60°F at Parshall on February 15, 1936

Average Annual Precipitation: 17 inches

Major Rivers: Cannonball, Goose, Heart, James, Knife, Little Missouri, Missouri, Park, Pembina, Red, Sheyenne, Souris

Major Lakes: Ashtabula, Devils, Horsehead, Long, Powers, Sakakawea, Stump, White

Trees: ash, aspen, basswood, box elder, elm, oak, poplar, willow

Wild Plants: beard-tongue, black-eyed Susan, bluegrass, buffalo grass, chokecherry, gaillardia, gama grass, pasqueflower, prairie mallow, red lily, wild plum, wild prairie rose

Animals: beaver, cottontail rabbit, coyote, deer, ground squirrel, jackrabbit, mink, prairie dog, pronghorn, raccoon, red fox, skunk, snowshoe rabbit, weasel

Jackrabbit

Birds: blackbird, duck, grouse, Hungarian partridge, magpie, oriole, quail, ring-necked pheasant, robin, sparrow, western meadowlark, wild turkey, wren

Fish: bass, catfish, crappie, northern pike, perch, walleye, sauger, sunfish, trout

Endangered Animals: black-footed ferret, Eskimo curlew, gray wolf, least tern, pallid sturgeon, whooping crane

Black-footed ferret

TIMELINE

North Dakota History

1600s Arikara, Hidatsa, Mandan, Ojibwa, and Sioux Indians live in what is now North Dakota

1682 France claims the lands drained by the Missouri River, including much of present-day North Dakota

1738 French explorer Pierre Gaultier de Varennes, Sieur de La Vérendrye, visits Mandan Indians living near the Missouri River, becoming the first European known to enter North Dakota

1781 North Dakota's first white-run business, a fur trading post, is built near the Souris River

1803 The United States gains most of North Dakota from France in the Louisiana Purchase

1804–1806 American explorers Meriwether Lewis and William Clark pass through North Dakota on their way to the Pacific Ocean and back, paving the way for future settlement

1812 Scottish and Irish settlers create North Dakota's first white farming community near Pembina

1818 The United States gains northeastern North Dakota from Great Britain; North Dakota becomes part of the Missouri Territory

1837 A smallpox epidemic nearly wipes out the Mandan Indians

1861 The U.S. government creates Dakota Territory

1863 Dakota Territory is opened to homesteading

1870 The Sioux and Ojibwa give up most of eastern North Dakota to the U.S. government

1876 The first "bonanza" wheat farm opens near Casselton, employing hundreds of men and boosting the region's economy

1881 The Northern Pacific Railroad completes a line across North Dakota

1889 North Dakota becomes the 39th state

1915 North Dakotans form the Nonpartisan League, a movement to support farmers

1919 The nation's only state-owned bank, the Bank of North Dakota, is founded

1922 A state-owned grain elevator and flour mill opens in Grand Forks

1930s A severe drought strikes North Dakota during the Great Depression; one-third of the state's farmers are forced to give up their land

1947 Theodore Roosevelt National Memorial Park is founded

1951 Oil is discovered near Tioga

1956 The Nonpartisan League merges with the Democratic Party; Garrison Dam is completed, forming Lake Sakakawea

1966 The most severe blizzard in North Dakota history strikes

1979 To boost the economy, the state government legalizes some forms of gambling

1988 North Dakota suffers its first major drought since the 1930s

1997 Severe flooding in the Red River valley forces 90 percent of the people in Grand Forks to leave their homes

ECONOMY

Agricultural Products: barley, beans, beef, canola seed, flaxseed, hogs, honey, oats, potatoes, rye, sugar beets, sunflower seeds, wheat

Hogs

Manufactured Products: computer disks, farm machinery, food products, petroleum products, transportation equipment, wood products

Natural Resources: clay, coal, lignite, natural gas, oil, sand and gravel, uranium

Business and Trade: healthcare, legal services, real estate, transportation, wholesale and retail trade

CALENDAR OF CELEBRATIONS

Winter Days West Fargo laughs at the cold during this weeklong festival in January, with an ice skating "olympics," a snow-golf tournament, and free sleigh rides.

Skydance Sakakawea At Fort Stevenson State Park, near Garrison, hundreds of kites of all shapes and sizes take to the air each May. Champion kite-flyers paint the sky red during three days of contests and demonstrations.

Grassy Butte Showdeo Young cowpokes from across the state compete at Western skills like barrel racing, goat tying, and calf riding during this junior rodeo in June.

Fort Seward Wagon Train For a genuine taste of the pioneer life, sign up for this June event near Jamestown. You'll head west for a week in a real covered wagon, learn frontier songs and stories, and camp out under the stars.

German Festival Street Fair New Leipzig celebrates its German heritage in July with music, dancing, and traditional foods like bratwurst (grilled sausage), káse knoepfla (cheese buttons), and pfeffernüss (spice cookies).

Taylor Horsefest You don't have to like horseback riding to enjoy this July celebration. Instead, you could win a prize tossing horseshoes, hitch a ride in a horse-drawn taxi, or watch powerful draft horses compete to see which team can pull the heaviest load.

Northern Plains Indian Culture Fest In late July, Native American artists demonstrate their skills at the Knife River Indian Villages near Stanton. Visitors can hear music played on a traditional flute or see beautiful designs made from porcupine quills.

Icelandic Celebration

Icelandic Celebration The first week in August, the town of Mountain rediscovers its Icelandic roots with a three-day festival featuring food, music, and dance from the Far North.

Nu'Eta Corn and Buffalo Festival This celebration of Mandan Indian culture takes place each August at Fort Abraham Lincoln State Park, near Mandan. Attractions include traditional dancing, crafts, and foods.

Enderlin Sunflower Festival The golden sunflower takes center stage at this harvest celebration in September, with events ranging from a seed-spitting contest to an old-fashioned tractor pull.

Stockcar Stampede North Dakota's biggest stockcar race is held each September in Jamestown, where daredevil drivers zoom around a track at breakneck speeds.

Makoti Threshing Show You'll see farmers threshing grain with old-time steam engines at this fall event. The country fun includes a pancake breakfast, a gospel sing-along, craft demonstrations, and two big parades.

Norsk Hostfest Folk musicians from Sweden, Denmark, Norway, and Iceland share the spotlight with some of America's biggest country stars at this October festival in Minot. Scandinavian treats like Swedish pancakes are another favorite attraction.

Dickens Village Festival As the holiday season starts in late November, folks in Garrison travel back in time to the world of 19th-century author Charles Dickens. Visitors can mingle with citizens dressed in old English costumes and take a tour of some of the town's oldest homes.

Old Fashioned Cowboy Christmas Each December Medora brings back North Dakota's frontier days with a shindig offering everything from Western music and dancing to a cowboy poker game.

STATE STARS

Maxwell Anderson (1888–1959) was one of America's most distinguished playwrights. Anderson, who was born in Pennsylvania, attended the University of North Dakota. He worked as a teacher and a reporter before turning to the theater full time. In 1924, he became a New York success with *What Price Glory*, a comedy about World War I. Many of his plays are about power and corruption in politics, including his 1933 drama *Both Your Houses*, which won a Pulitzer Prize.

Maxwell Anderson

Warren Christopher

Warren Christopher (1925–   ) is a leading statesman. Christopher served as deputy secretary of state under President Jimmy Carter and as secretary of state under President Bill Clinton. Under Carter, he helped negotiate the return of 52 Americans taken hostage at the U.S. embassy in Iran. Because of that achievement, he was awarded the Medal of Freedom in 1981. Christopher was born in Scranton.

Angie Dickinson (1931–   ) is an actress best known for playing a tough, smart detective in the 1970s television show *Police Woman*. A native of Kulm, Dickinson has appeared in more than 50 film and television productions.

Angie Dickinson

Carl Ben Eielson (1897–1929) was a pioneering aviator and Arctic explorer. Born and raised in Hatton, Eielson learned to fly after joining the army in 1917. He later moved to Fairbanks, Alaska, where he went into business flying people and supplies across the Far North. Eielson made a nonstop flight over the North Pole in 1928. A year later, he was killed in a crash while coming to the aid of a ship off Alaska's shores.

Louise Erdrich (1954–   ) is a novelist, poet, and short story writer known for her vivid characters and Native American themes. Erdrich, who is part Ojibwa, grew up in Wahpeton, where her parents worked at the Bureau of Indian Affairs school. Many of her best-known books, including *Love Medicine* and *The Bingo Palace*, take place on the North Dakota plains.

Phyllis Frelich (1944–   ) is an actress who has helped open the world of theater to the hearing-impaired. The oldest of nine deaf children, Frelich grew up on a farm near Devils Lake and began performing as a college student in Washington, D.C. She helped found the National Theater for the Deaf in the 1960s, and in 1981 she won a Tony Award for her performance in the Broadway play *Children of a Lesser God*.

Phil Jackson (1945–   ) played basketball with the New York Knicks and went on to become one of the game's most successful coaches. Jackson was a high school basketball star in Williston and later played for the University of North Dakota. After 13 years in the NBA he eventually became head coach of the Chicago Bulls, leading the team to six national championships in nine years. Jackson's quiet but powerful coaching style later won him a contract with the Los Angeles Lakers.

Louis L'Amour (1908–1988), a native of Jamestown, was a popular Western fiction writer. L'Amour tried everything from logging to mining to professional boxing before settling down to write full time. In 35 years, he wrote more than a hundred novels, won the Congressional Gold Medal and Presidential Medal of Freedom, and received a Spur Award for his bestseller *Down the Long Hills*.

William L. Langer (1886–1959) was one of North Dakota's most controversial politicians. A strong leader with a colorful personality, he was elected governor in 1932. Langer's bold measures gave hope to farmers during the Great Depression, but in 1934 he was convicted of campaign violations and removed from office. Two years later that decision was overturned, and Langer was reelected. He went on to serve in the U.S. Senate from 1941 until his death in 1959.

William L. Langer

Peggy Lee (1920–   ) is a singer and songwriter who rose to fame with the great swing bands of the 1940s and 1950s. Lee was born in Jamestown and got an early start singing for a radio station in Fargo. Discovered by bandleader Benny Goodman in 1941, her cool, smoky voice soon made her a national star. Lee helped write many of her own numbers, including the hits "It's a Good Day" and "Mañana."

Roger Maris (1934–1985) made baseball history by passing Babe Ruth's single-season home run record. Raised in Fargo, where he played football as well as baseball, Maris was named the American League's Most Valuable Player twice and led his teams to the World Series seven times. But his greatest moment came in 1961, when he hit his 61st home run of the year on the last day of the season, topping Ruth's legendary 60 homers of 1927.

Casper Oimoen (1906–1995), who moved from Norway to Minot when he was 17, was a world-class skier and ski jumper. A three-time national ski-jumping champion and 1936 captain of the Olympic ski team, Oimoen was inducted into the U.S. Skiing Hall of Fame in 1963. He was a bricklayer by trade and helped build the state capitol in Bismarck.

James Rosenquist (1933–   ) a Grand Forks native, played a major role in the pop art movement of the 1960s. After working as a billboard painter, Rosenquist continued to create art on a gigantic scale. Images of modern life from weapons to household products make up his enormous paintings. One of the best known, *F-lll*, is more than 80 feet wide.

James Rosenquist

Sacagawea (1786?–1812) helped guide explorers Meriwether Lewis and William Clark as they blazed a trail to the Pacific Ocean. Sacagawea was a Shoshone Indian who was taken captive by another tribe while still a child. She became the wife of a French fur trapper, and the two joined Lewis and Clark near what is now Bismarck, North Dakota. The only woman on the expedition, she helped the group travel through Shoshone lands.

Eric Sevareid (1912–1992) was one of the most respected journalists in radio and television. Born in Velva, Severeid became a radio reporter. His dramatic reports from Europe grabbed the nation's attention during World War II. Moving to televison, he reached the peak of his career as a commentator on *The CBS Evening News*.

Eric Sevareid

Era Bell Thompson (1906–1986) was a journalist known for her skilled reporting on black issues in the United States and around the world. Thompson was born in Iowa but moved to a farm near Driscoll when she was five. After graduating from the University of North Dakota she worked her way up in journalism, and in 1964 she became the international editor for *Ebony* magazine. Her autobiography, *American Daughter*, describes her childhood in North Dakota.

Bobby Vee (1943–   ), a singer and songwriter from Fargo, made the top of the pop charts at age 16 with his single "Suzie Baby." After recording

two more number-one songs with his rocka-
billy band the Shadows, Vee produced hits
on his own throughout the 1960s. His gold
records include "Devil or Angel" and "Take
Good Care of My Baby."

Bobby Vee

Lawrence Welk (1903–1992) hosted television's most popular "golden
oldies" program for more than twenty years. Welk grew up in a sod house
near Strasburg, where he broke into show business playing accordian
for local dances. After his first television appearance in 1955, he enter-
tained millions with his "champagne orchestra," a group that recalled the
big bands of days gone by.

Lawrence Welk

Larry Woiwode (1941–   ) is an award-winning poet, novelist, and short story writer. Although he published his first works of literature while living in New York City in the 1960s, two of his best-known books, *Beyond the Bedroom Wall* and *Born Brothers*, describe the desolate beauty of North Dakota. Woiwode grew up in Sykeston and now lives on a farm near Mott.

TOUR THE STATE

Theodore Roosevelt National Park (Medora) Hiking trails lead past huge, colorful rock formations in this 110-square-mile stretch of the badlands.

Bonanzaville U.S.A. (West Fargo) Historic buildings including a one-room schoolhouse, a jail, and an old-fashioned general store take visitors back to the days of the pioneers.

Lake Sakakawea North Dakota's largest lake was created when Garrison Dam was built. Its cool waters make it a haven for swimming, boating, and fishing all summer long.

Fort Union Trading Post (Williston) An 18-foot stockade surrounds the spot where Native Americans from across the plains met white fur traders to exchange buffalo and beaver pelts for guns and metal tools.

Children's Museum at Yunker Farm (Fargo) The exhibits at this kids' museum include a giant honeycomb and a display of live bees.

Writing Rock (Grenora) Two granite boulders here are covered with ancient Native American petroglyphs—pictures the Indians used to leave messages behind.

Dakota Dinosaur Museum

Dakota Dinosaur Museum (Dickinson) Prehistoric beasts like triceratops once roamed the badlands. Some of their enormous skeletons are on display near their original home.

International Peace Garden (Dunseith) The dazzling flowers, sparkling pools, and elegant pathways of this formal garden celebrate the friendship between the United States and Canada. The park sits right on the border between the two countries and halfway between the east and west coasts.

Turtle Mountain Chippewa Heritage Center (Belcourt) At this museum on the Turtle Mountain Indian Reservation, you can learn about the history and culture of the Ojibwa Indians.

Pfenning Wildlife Museum (Beulah) On the outside this place looks like a castle from the Middle Ages. Inside is an amazing animal display, featuring stuffed exotic creatures from around the world.

Knife River Indian Villages (Stanton) Hidatsa Indians lived on the banks of the Knife and Missouri Rivers for more than 500 years. You can still see where their villages stood because their lodges left marks in the soil.

Chateau de Mores State Historic Site (Medora) The frontier town of Medora was built by a French nobleman known as the Marquis de Mores. His family spent summers in this lavish mansion, which now offers guided tours.

Five Nations Arts (Mandan) The work of more than 200 Native American artists is on display at this cultural center, dedicated to the Mandan, Hidatsa, Arikara, Ojibwa, and Sioux tribes.

Little Missouri National Grassland (Belfield) The prairies, valleys, and craggy buttes of this vast preserve are teeming with wildlife, from bighorn sheep to prairie dogs.

North Dakota Heritage Center (Bismarck) The history of the Great Plains comes to life at this museum, where you can tour a buffalo-hide tepee or examine the remains of an ancient mastadon.

Bagg Bonanza Farm (Mooreton) North Dakota's last surviving bonanza wheat farm is a reminder of the bold spirit that made the state strong.

Plains Art Museum (Fargo) Works by artists from the prairie states are presented here, from traditional Native American arts to modern sculpture, drawings, and paintings.

Des Lacs National Wildlife Refuge (Kenmare) The lakes and wetlands along this beautiful stretch of the Des Lacs River valley attract thousands of wild ducks, geese, grebes, and pelicans.

National Buffalo Museum (Jamestown) This North Dakota landmark boasts its own herd of live buffalo. Exhibits tell about the evolution of the beast and how it fed and clothed Plains Indians.

FUN FACTS

The world's largest hamburger was eaten in Rutland in 1982. More than 8,000 people were invited to the meal, which weighed 3,591 pounds.

Most of the pasta produced in the United States is made from North Dakota durum wheat. Grand Forks holds a huge pasta party each year in honor of the crop.

In the 1930s, Max G. Taubert, the owner of a gas station and truck stop in Casselton, built a pyramid of oil cans 50 feet high. Known for serving the best hamburgers between Chicago and Seattle, Taubert's place is closed today, but the Can Pile monument still stands.

FIND OUT MORE

Would you like to learn more about North Dakota? Here are some suggestions for where to start.

GENERAL STATE BOOKS

Fradin, Dennis Brindell. *North Dakota*. New York: Children's Press, 1998.

Hintz, Martin. *North Dakota*. New York: Children's Press, 2000.

SPECIAL INTEREST BOOKS

Bial, Raymond. *The Sioux*. Tarrytown, NY: Marshall Cavendish, 1998.

Blumberg, Rhoda. *The Incredible Journey of Lewis and Clark*. New York: Lathrop, Lee & Shepard, 1987.

Schneider, Mary Jane. *The Hidatsa*. New York: Chelsea House, 1989.

Silverman, Robin Landew. *A Bosnian Family* (Journey Between Two Worlds series). Minneapolis: Lerner, 1997.

WEBSITES

www.state.nd.us
  The official website of the state of North Dakota

www.lib.ndsu.nodak.edu/reference/ndakota
  Includes links to sites on history, geography, sports, and many other topics

INDEX

Page numbers for charts, graphs, and illustrations are in boldface.